The Dark Side of the Mind

Stories of love, courage and transformation

Alba Alamillo
Certified Hypnotherapist

To Jared, my love.

Table of Contents

Introduction

This book is about the contradictions that we find in our mind: We want to achieve something important to us, fulfill a dream, reach a goal but then ... we get the absolute opposite. It can be to get a better job, lose weight, go to the gym, do our taxes on time, stop watching so much TV or register for a class we want to take.

For many people, achieving their goals is very difficult and every New Year is the same thing, the same resolutions over and over. We start off excited; with a list of *I want*s only to find a couple of months later that once again, it didn't work out.

The goal of this book is to explain the hidden part of the mind that doesn't want to help you achieve your goals, wishes or dreams. I will explain why this *hidden* mind tends to sabotage your progress, and I will provide you with the tools to make that mind your ally instead of your adversary.

Let me give you a simple example of this dynamic between the part of you that wants to achieve something, and the other one that—like a stubborn child—just doesn't want to cooperate.

This past January, I went to the mall to shop at the end-of-year sales. I found beautiful things at amazing prices. Every time I saw a nice outfit my mind would say "Wow, that's elegant, I want it!" And I would get some of the things I liked. The outfits I bought were very nice and elegant indeed.

"I want to look nice and elegant," I thought, therefore I bought elegant clothes and I took them home. When I was hanging them in the closet, I realized that *I already* had nice, new and unworn elegant clothes. That's when it hit me and I realized the difference between the *I want* and the *I am*.

I want to look elegant but ... *I am not* an elegant woman.

Who *am I* then?

I am a practical woman who loves flexibility and comfort. I like clothes that feel nice and allow me to move around and go places easily, like a t-shirt, a pair of jeans and flat shoes. Therefore, every morning, when choosing the clothes to wear, I choose them based on who *I am*: a practical woman. There's consistency between my choices and my definition of who I am, and that's great because the mind likes coherence.

"But *I want* to be elegant!" one little voice says inside my mind. "Go ahead, Alba! Wear that silk blouse and those high heels!"

"No" the *I am* voice says. "The blouse will get dirty when I wash the dishes, I also have a meeting at my son's school. If I wear that, they will ask me what the occasion is. I also have to walk a lot; I cannot handle high heels today. Maybe some other time."

And that happens every day, because every day I make an excuse to be what I have always been: *practical.*

And I make a good excuse not to be what *I want* to be: *elegant*.

The *I am* will always overpower the *I want*.

Let's take the New Year's resolution that everybody makes:

"*I want* to start going to the gym (this year *for sure*)"

But many of the people I know, who want to go to the gym and end up not going don't define themselves as the "athletic type." They define themselves as a "lazy bum."

I am a lazy bum, but ... *I want* to go to the gym.

Every morning, they will have this mental debate. Their to-do list is packed with busy activities, except any type of exercise, and even when the little *I want* voice screams that it wants to go the gym, the *I am* voice takes over and tells it to be reasonable.

"Yes, I know *you want* that, but today I have breakfast with friends, after that I have to bring snacks to the school party, I have to pick up the kids, help with the homework, cook dinner, watch some TV with my husband, and then go to sleep. Maybe tomorrow."

Tomorrow comes, and the *I want* voice insists that it *wants* to go to the gym, that there's time today. But the *I am* voice will come up with another excuse of why exercise is not an option again: "Yes, you are right. Today I have time, but I am tired and need to rest."

At some point the *I want* voice will stop asking because the *I am* voice always wins. The *I am* statement is ingrained in our DNA, our pores, our skin, our heart, our personality. It's in the way we walk, the way we talk, the way we communicate with others, the way we react, the way we dress, the food we eat, the friends we have and the decisions we make. On the other hand, the *I want* is alien. It's not here; it's there, behind a glass display.

This book will help you establish coherence between the *I want* and the *I am,* so that when you want to achieve something, the *I am* will be with you and not against you, sabotaging you every step of the way.

*   *   *

Now that we are talking about *I am's*, let me introduce myself.

I am a woman who has lived in the Bay Area in California since 2001, and I am originally from Mexico City. I live with my husband Jared and my two teenage sons. I'm a hypnotherapist, a life coach and a career consultant.

In addition to being passionate about the human mind and behaviors, I'm also crafty, which makes me Pinterest's number one fan. I love making colorful glycerin and cold-process soaps and baking.

My baking specialty is scones. (The best in the menu are bacon and chocolate chip—and yes, they are to die for—sorry Starbucks, but when someone tries my scones they don't want to buy yours any more). [1]

I was raised in Mexico City, surrounded by an extended family that got together frequently. Those family reunions made me become interested in human interactions and psychological games. I loved listening to people's problems and I was my dolls' first (and maybe last) shrink.

When I was twelve, my mom handed me the book *Your Erroneous Zones* by Wayne Dyer, and that's when the adventure started—I fell in love with the topic of self-esteem, goals and human relationships. That's all I read and all I have read for the last 30 years.

My reading interests are extremely focused. Sometimes, just to get out of my comfort zone, I read something else like a novel or a non-fiction book about a different topic, only to discover that I'll fall asleep in less than thirty seconds.

By the time I was thirteen, I had already read so many books that I wrote my own 40-page booklet using my dad's typewriter and fixing the typos with liquid paper. (If you are under 20 you probably have no idea what I'm talking about.) It looks more like a relic than like a book.

For the last twenty years. I've been talking to people about their inner thoughts and feelings, about the things that they don't share with anyone else because they find them too embarrassing or sad. I know a lot about insecurities, feelings of worthlessness, passive-aggressive behavior, low self-esteem, relationship issues, manipulation, deception, narcissistic behavior, shame, love, hate, resentment, anxiety, depression, and procrastination. The interaction with my clients has been very rich and intellectually challenging, and I have learned much more from our conversations than from books. I love what I do and I truly care for my clients.

---

[1] If you want the scones recipe I can give it to you. Just send me an e-mail.

The clients' names in this book are all fictitious (except for the name of my children, husband and dogs) and each story is a mixture of several clients' tales, as their privacy is very important to me.

My love for the human mind has grown over the years, and my goal is to share my expertise with you, hoping that it will help you achieve the goals that are dear to your heart but that you haven't been able to achieve.

Chapter 1

How your Belief System (the *I am*) is Created?

"No two persons can learn something and experience it in the same way."

Shannon Alder

Let's start by talking about the *I am,* which is determined by your belief system.

Your belief system is a combination of all the beliefs you hold in your head about life, how you see yourself, how you see others, what you like, what you dislike, what makes you happy, what soothes you, what makes you sad or angry, what you love or what you hate.

The *I am* is the belief of who you think you are: as a husband, wife, son, daughter, mother, father, friend, student, teacher, professional, etc.

The *I want* is what you don't have but you wish you did. You can want a lot of things, such as: To be confident, go to the gym, eat healthier or get promoted.

Our belief system is created by our surroundings, the lessons we've learned, the situations we've lived and, believe it or not, *our interpretation of those situations*. That's why each person's belief system is different, even if they live in the same environment at the same time.

For example: A frustrated mom yells at her identical twin sons, Mike and Leo.

Mike takes offense, feels embarrassed and ashamed. In the meantime, Leo notices that while his mom was yelling, her gestures were very funny, like the cartoon he watched the day before. "Oh gosh!" he thinks, "My mom looks like SpongeBob when she's angry! That is so funny! And Mike's face is funny, too!" Mike is holding back the tears while Leo is holding back the laughter: same event, different interpretations.

There are random events in your life that don't become part of your belief system, because they are not meaningful enough. For example, when you are working on a project and there's a small fly bugging you, you just shoo it away and that's that. Another example could be the person in front of you at the grocery store, who just pays and leaves without making too much fuss, the lights in the room you are in, or the pitch of the voice of the people you talk to. Those events don't have an emotional impact and the mind doesn't store them with the same care as it does the relevant ones.

Interesting fact: *The theories that say that our brain stores every single memory we've had since the moment we were born—and maybe even before—are wrong. People used to think that with hypnosis it was possible to 'rewind' every experience from any point in our lives. People say they can remember things in hypnosis, but those memories will be false. If I hypnotize you and ask you to remember your fifth birthday party, you will tell me all the details about the clowns, your guests, the cake, the presents etc. But if I ask your mom, she will tell me a complete different story: She remembers your fifth birthday really well because everybody was in bed with the flu. Those false memories are called confabulation, and we confabulate much more than we realize or want to admit.*

Still, the mind stores information, and the key concern for the mind is this: Is the information meaningful? Then let's store it. Is it irrelevant? Then let's delete it. We will cover in later chapters how the mind is actually an expert at deleting information. That brings us to the next question: How does the mind decide what's meaningful versus what's not?

By repetition and shock (or sometimes both).

1. Repetition: If an idea, experience or stimulus is repeated over and over and over—it will become meaningful. These experiences or ideas can be happy, sad, embarrassing, enlightening, or terrifying.

2. Shock: If an idea, experience or stimulus happens only once but has emotional impact—it will become meaningful. These experiences or ideas can be happy, sad, embarrassing, enlightening, or terrifying.

The meaningful ideas are stored in the long-term memory compartment, and the not-so-meaningful ones will be stored in the short-term memory compartment and may be forgotten.

The mind loves compartments and labels, because the sooner the mind can associate something (a bee, a red light, a cookie) with something else (that bees sting and we should avoid them, that we need to press the breaks at a red light, that cookies bring us pleasure), the better equipped we are to protect ourselves from danger. Therefore an isolated event with no explanation whatsoever, will create confusion. We'll talk about labels and compartments later.

Another aspect of the mind that you probably already know is that our mind has two important parts: Subconscious and Conscious.

Subconscious mind. It's where the *I am* is stored. It controls the automatic reactions of your body like blinking, breathing swallowing, the proper functioning of your organs and many others. When you are driving and the car in front of you suddenly stops, you automatically slam your breaks. You don't have enough time to sit and ponder about the situation and gauge the pros and cons of stopping. You simply do it. That reaction is called the fight-or-flight response, and it's triggered when your survival is compromised. I also believe that our gut feelings, intuition and sudden sparks of inspiration come from it. Throughout this book, I will call it either subconscious mind or emotional brain.

Conscious mind. It's where the *I want* and willpower come from. It's in charge of our decision-making process and it's located in the outer layer of the brain called the neocortex. This means that from an evolutionary point of view, this part of the brain was added much later than the rest. I will call this mind the conscious mind or the logical brain.

Both parts have more abilities and power than I will describe in this book, but I will simply cover what's relevant to our decision making process and belief system. In a nutshell, the logical brain or conscious mind decides. And the subconscious mind or emotional brain reacts.

Interesting fact: *Even though the neocortex (host of the conscious mind) is much larger than the limbic system (host of the subconscious mind), the subconscious is much more powerful than the conscious. The mental power of the subconscious mind is approximately 85% of all brain power, while the conscious mind has barely 15%. Why is the emotional brain smaller but still more powerful? Because one of the mind's traits is that it loves to be economical and to save resources. More mass doesn't necessarily mean more power. So, if there's a discrepancy of opinions between the two, your subconscious mind will wipe poor little logic away.*

Disclaimer: I cannot tell for a fact the exact boundaries between the conscious and subconscious minds in the geography of the brain. There may be parts of the subconscious brain that are located in the neocortex and vice-versa. I believe it will remain a mystery until Google Maps does something about it.

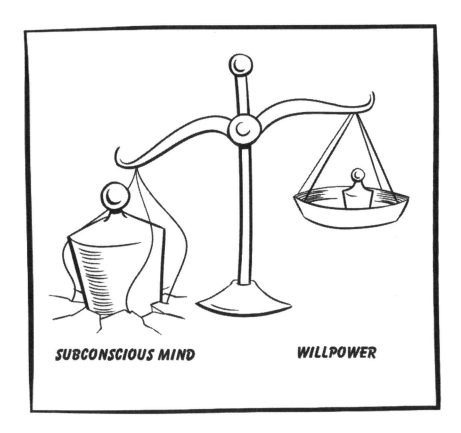

SUBCONSCIOUS MIND   WILLPOWER

A phobia created by shock

One of my clients was in a car accident and got really scared. The emotional impact was more significant than the collision, and after that, he developed a phobia of driving. Since his accident was emotionally traumatic for him, I'll call that a *shock*. Phobias are not logical and are buried in the subconscious mind. In his case, a new belief was formed: "Cars are too dangerous and I cannot drive."

Now he cannot drive a car without feeling panic and losing control (fight-or-flight).

> *"The fight-or-flight response, also known as the acute stress response, refers to a physiological reaction that occurs in the presence of something that is terrifying, either mentally or*

physically. The fight-or-flight response was first described in the 1920s by American physiologist Walter Cannon. Cannon realized that a chain of rapidly occurring reactions inside the body help mobilize the body's resources to deal with threatening circumstances."

www.psychology.about.com

My client uses his logical mind to persuade himself: "It doesn't make sense to me. I have driven all my life and now I cannot get in a car without feeling anxious. Something must be extremely wrong with me."

"Nothing is wrong. Actually, everything is right." I say.

(A little offended) "What do you mean, everything is right? I need to drive places and now my wife has to take me everywhere. If everything was right as you say, I would be able to drive."

"The subconscious mind's goal is to keep you safe. The accident made your mind believe that cars aren't safe and since it thinks that your survival is compromised, it will create a phobia to keep you out of trouble." And logic can try all it wants, it won't convince the subconscious mind, no matter how much it begs, whines or reasons.

If your subconscious mind could talk, it would say something like this: "If you are in danger, I will make sure that you are safe. My goal is not to have you like me or help you drive. My goal is to make sure you stay away from danger."

A phobia created by repetition

I had another client with a phobia of driving. In her case it was repetition instead of shock, even though after meeting her I made the obvious assumption: "She probably was in a car accident."

I was wrong. Then I considered the second reason, repetition.

"What are your beliefs about cars and driving?" I asked.

Her beliefs were that cars are extremely unsafe. She was raised by her grandmother, who told her throughout her childhood that cars were very dangerous. When she became an adult and learned how to drive, she discovered that the moment she got behind the wheel her anxiety was unbearable. She had the thought "cars are very dangerous" over and over and over and over (*repetition*). She dwelled on it so much that suddenly she found herself with a phobia of driving. Her phobia was as strong as the guy who was in a real car accident.

Interesting fact: *Suppose that you are lost in a city, you don't know where you are or how you got there. But you have a GPS in your hand. You can enter the address of your destination and follow the route. Wondering about how you got there won't help you move towards your destination. The reason I say this is because some clients want me to do a 'hypnotic age regression.' They want to find out what happened to them in their childhood. They believe that finding out how they got there is the key to knowing how to get out. That isn't true. It isn't necessary that we remember what kind of repetitions and shocks we experienced as children in order to gain more confidence or achieve our goals. I tell them what I'm telling you now: All you need is a GPS, not a dissertation describing your past.*

How it all started for all of us

Let's analyze a random baby named Charlie to understand how our belief system is created.

When Charlie is born, he has at least 100 billion neurons available to learn about his environment; the neurons that are not used will die, and the ones that are used will start making connections. We start creating our belief system the moment we are born, perhaps even before. Charlie will learn in his younger years what is safe versus what is not, what causes sadness, anger, pain, loneliness, joy, laughter, etc.

Babies like Charlie perceive their world through their senses: what mom and dad look like, if there's an older sibling or a family pet, what it feels like to be held, what milk tastes like, the sound of the voices around them. Charlie is born with only two fears: loud noises and being dropped. Every other fear will be learned.

As Charlie becomes a toddler and then a boy, those brain connections keep on forming. Any meaningful event will make two isolated neurons trigger an electrical or a chemical reaction. These reactions join the neurons so they can exchange information. If those receptors are repeatedly stimulated over time, a physical connection will be created. That connection is called a neural pathway. A neural pathway takes less energy than two isolated neurons firing. This happens for the same reasons I talked about before: The brain is serious about saving resources.

Let's assume that when Charlie is born he meets three people: his parents and the nice nurse who works at the hospital where he is delivered. In those few days at the hospital, he will probably interact with the three of them, and he will associate their faces with feelings of being happy, protected and cared for (hopefully). "These three people seem nice. I feel safe when I am with them." Three neural pathways are created. Two are called, "Being with mom/dad feels nice" and the other one is called, "Being with the nurse feels nice."

Finally, he goes home. The nurse is no longer a part of his life, but mom and dad stay. The neural pathways called "Being with mom/dad feels nice" are constantly reinforced—*repetition*—which makes that brain connection stronger.

He will start to forget about the nurse and that old connection becomes weak. At some point in his life, he can have a casual encounter with that nurse and seeing her may trigger a little smile in his lips, but he won't know why.

Interesting fact: *What we think about chemistry is wrong; it's just a way to describe something that's indescribable. When we like or dislike somebody, that's because our mental files associate that person's tone of voice, body language, smell, hairstyle, clothing,* *laughter or gestures with something similar in our past that brought us happiness or pain. Maybe this guy has spiky hair like your first grade teacher's (even when you consciously don't remember that), and you think there's chemistry between you and him. But unfortunately, your scent reminds him of the aunt he hated the most. (Even if he doesn't consciously remember it.) Then, when I secretly ask you: "Why did you like him?" you won't be able to put your finger on why, and if I ask him: "Why didn't you like her?" he won't be able to give me a logical explanation either. That's when the word "chemistry" comes in handy. He'll probably excuse himself by saying: "it's not her, it's me." But it's neither. It's the aunt.*

A baby is more aware of his or her world than we can imagine. We only see them eat, sleep, cry and poop. But they are absorbing more information than we would expect.

Let's suppose that around Christmas time his mom is walking through the mall with him and she realizes that Santa is there, being photographed with the children.

"Oh Charlie look! Your first Christmas! Let's take a picture with Santa!"

His interpretation of the events can vary between:

"This funny-looking fellow seems nice," therefore he giggles for the picture, and:

"My mom is giving me away to this strange looking guy!" Therefore he cries his lungs out. That's why, if you pay attention in the shopping mall around Christmas, you'll see some toddlers running joyfully towards Santa, waiting impatiently for their turn to sit on his lap, while others will run too... but in the opposite direction.

Everything is a matter of personal perception.

As Charlie and you were growing up, you both absorbed all the information around you and tried to make sense of it. Your subconscious mind needed to sort out what was a happy experience versus a sad one, so you could seek out happier experiences and avoid sad ones. You learned that Santa was scary, that mom was nice, that hugs felt good, that your dad's frown meant disapproval, that stoves burned little hands, that electric outlets shocked, that family reunions were tiring, and that cookies made everything better.

Some more examples of repetition

When you get a new phone number and need to remember it, you practice saying it over and over until you memorize it and it becomes automatic. A neural pathway is created.

The cute little thing in the picture is me, even when Santa didn't seem to agree.

After you change your phone number, the neural connection of the old phone number will become weaker, and you may forget it at some point.

Here are other examples of things that we learn through repetition: the multiplication tables, driving, playing an instrument, the route to work, the pattern you follow when brushing your teeth.

Sadly, you also accept things you are told over and over … like you were not a good little boy or girl.

If as a child you were constantly told that you were dumb, you'd probably find it difficult to get rid of that feeling of 'dumbness' (*repetition*).

Examples of shock

Your mom puts you on the lap of someone scary and after that, every person similar in any way to him will make you frown. After a dog bites you, you develop a dog phobia; you have a car accident and you become terrified of driving; somebody behaves in a cruel or offensive manner and therefore you get anxious every time you see that person.

There can also be happy shocks

Your uncle picks you up and tosses you high in the air, catching you while you laugh hysterically. After that, you feel excited every time you see him. You win a popularity contest in school, and then you get a major self-esteem boost. Your boss praises you in front of the owners of the company that you work for, and then you feel happy and perform better.

Or, maybe no one called you dumb, but one time something happened to you that made you so embarrassed (*shock*) that now you feel dumb almost all the time.

If our ancestors hadn't learned important information, through either repetition or shock, they would have compromised their survival.

The subconscious mind's job is to store as much relevant information as it can because its goal is to keep you safe. Your beliefs are stored in your mind and they will remain there happily ever after. Your whole system will reject your efforts to try to change it. But it's doable.

Your subconscious mind doesn't like change in general, let alone if the change is associated with the *I am,* because if the well-known *I am* has kept you alive in the past, your subconscious won't make it easy for you to change it. What if the new *I am* jeopardizes your safety?

When you were a child, your mother gave you a cookie when you fell off your bike and scratched your knee. That felt really good.

Cookie + happy emotion = New belief: cookies are good!

Birthday parties were fun and full of cookies, ice cream and cake.

Sweets + happy emotions + soothing + nice people + repetitions (many birthday parties during your childhood) = Sweets are good!

Cookies, sweets, cakes and candy are associated with fun and with nice people.

Then, as an adult, you get new information because the doctor tells you that you have to lower your sugar intake. Your logical mind cares, but your subconscious mind won't budge.

An internal dialog goes like this:

Logical mind: "Hey, I just went to the doctor, I need to reduce the amount of sugar I eat!"

Subconscious mind: "Sure, give me a second" ... and it looks in its mental files and realizes that all the associations you have with sweets are positive. "Sorry, I don't see any threat here, all the opposite, only happiness, soothing, birthday parties and hugs."

Logical mind: "But the doctor says!"

Subconscious mind: "I cannot help you, sorry."

Logical mind: "Fine! I'll use my willpower then!"

And you use your willpower, but the subconscious mind will make sure it sabotages you over and over because you are challenging a belief that is set in stone.

Here's another example from my clients:

As children, they were punished and yelled at (*shock*) if they defied their parents or teachers. They learned to be a good boy or girl who never argued with authority. Then, those kids grow older and guess what happens when they want to climb the corporate ladder, when they want to voice their opinions, when they need to make a presentation, when they have to say something at company meetings.

TWO WAYS TO CREATE A BELIEF:

THROUGH REPETITION

THROUGH SHOCK

This is what happens: absolutely nothing.

They learned to be good children, to be seen but not heard, to not argue or question the adults in their lives. Their parents always bragged to their friends about how lucky they were to have such quiet, obedient and docile children.

Now those enviable children are adults and their conscious mind has a hard time explaining to the subconscious that they are adults now, that they should speak up, ask for a raise, voice their opinions and even argue if needed.

Logical mind: "I need to feel calm when I have to speak in meetings."

Subconscious mind: "Sure, let me check the files for you … one second … Wait a moment! Here it says that in order for you to stay out of trouble you have to be seen but not heard, that you have to be liked by the adults around you, and never argue."

Logical mind: "Yes, but many of those adults that I have to deal with now are even younger than me."

Subconscious mind: "I believe you, but that doesn't change the fact that they are adults and that you are supposed to be good and quiet around them."

As you can see, common sense is not one of the subconscious mind's best attributes. Keeping you safe is.

That *good-boy* belief keeps them from asking for a promotion or asserting themselves when needed. That belief makes them freeze and panic. Some of them don't follow their dreams, for fear of disappointing their peers or bosses.

If a phobia or fear is not treated with *repetition* or *shock* (the same way it was created) it will stay there.

*   *   *

When I was little, my parents used to take me to my uncle's house. It was a house with a sliding garage door, so anyone could go inside. They had a beautiful, playful English sheepdog named Waldo. He was never locked up and as we entered the house I could see him running towards us, jumping for joy. Since I was small and Waldo was big and strong, he would knock me down and pin me to the floor and lick my face. That was a terrifying experience for me (*shock*) that happened almost every time that we visited my uncle (*repetition*).

Rationally, I knew that Waldo was not dangerous and that he was a sweet dog, but that didn't keep me from feeling terrified. Now, as an adult, if I happen to see an English sheepdog, I can instantly feel a cringe in my stomach. That doesn't happen with other breeds even if they are bigger than an English sheepdog. I haven't done anything about this phobia because it doesn't affect my daily life.

If you live in America and you have a phobia of unleashed kangaroos you don't have a problem, but if you are afraid of driving, you do. You should work on changing the beliefs that interfere with your goals, not with every single negative belief you have.

Catching the baseball

When a pattern is ignored and a new pattern is created, the mind forces itself to adapt after the new pattern has proven itself to be important.

Imagine that you are in a park, sitting relaxed on a bench, enjoying the day and suddenly... SHOOOSHHHH! a baseball is about to hit you in the face! Your automatic reaction is to grab the ball or duck, even before you consciously realize that there is a ball coming your way. There's no time for your conscious mind to calculate the speed and direction of the ball, no time to wonder if you should duck, move to the right, to the left or catch it, no time for you to lick your index finger and stick it out to check the direction in which the wind is blowing. You just catch it. Period.

Now, imagine that I have that same baseball in my hand and I tell you that I will simply 'pretend' to throw it at your face, that I will make the whole professional baseball pitcher swing, but I won't let go of the ball. I promise you that and you believe me (your logical brain believes me; your subconscious mind doesn't because it doesn't have the magic ingredients of repetition or shock). I thrust my hand towards your face and your automatic reaction will be to cover your face to protect it, even though I told you that I was not going to let go of the ball. Why would you do that if you truly believe me?

Because your conscious and subconscious mind are having a dialog similar to the one they had when the doctor told you to lower your sugar intake.

Logical mind: "Alba just told me that she will pretend to toss a ball to hit me on the face and I believe her. I want to remain still as if nothing was happening."

Subconscious mind: "Sure, no problem."

So, then here I am making the perfect professional pitcher swing, pretending to throw the ball at your face, but I don't let go of the ball. Still you blink and feel an impulse in your hands to protect your face.

Logical mind: "Hey! I told you not to move! Or blink! Or hold your breath! Aren't you listening?"

Subconscious mind: "Yes, yes, but it looked so real, and you know, for me, safety first."

Here I go again, making the swing, now you blink and feel the impulse but it's weaker. And I do it again, and your reaction becomes less intense. Your instinct to grab the ball will get weaker because we are creating a new belief that states, "When Alba *pretends* to throw the ball, nothing will happen and I am safe." I'll do it so many times *(repetition)* that eventually you won't even blink. The old neural pathway (belief) becomes dormant, and a new one is created. You have successfully inhibited your body's reaction to my arm movement.

Now, what if I come by surprise and throw the ball at your face? It will hit you because you will not react to the movement of my arm, and very likely the subconscious mind will tell the conscious mind "I told you so."

Then the old belief of, "If somebody throws a ball at my face" will rise from the ashes.

This is something that I tell my clients and I tell you now:

YOU CAN WEAKEN OLD NEURAL PATHWAYS, EVEN ONES THAT HAVE BEEN WITH YOU FOR A VERY LONG TIME. IT DOESN'T MATTER IF YOU HAVE HAD THAT BELIEF FOR THE LAST FIFTY YEARS, YOU CAN CHANGE IT.

Interesting fact: *When an older person tells you "Nahhh, I'm too old to change" what he actually means is: "I really don't know if I can change or not, but I don't care, because I don't want to change so I'll use my age as an excuse."*

Neuroplasticity

In his book *The Power of Habit*, Charles Duhigg talks about the brain scans of one woman, Lisa Allen, who dramatically changed her life situation. She was overweight, smoked frequently, and was constantly in debt. That's when the first brain scan was taken. A few years later, Lisa made serious changes in her life. She had lost all the extra weight, was fit, ran marathons, was debt-free, and had quit smoking. She also had a new job and was recently promoted. She had new brain scans taken. To everyone's surprise, her brain didn't look like the pictures of her previous scan. It was as if it were a different person's brain. Some new neural pathways were created and some were almost non-existent, which allowed the doctors to come to the conclusion that we are able to physically—YES physically—change our brain connections anytime if our brain is generally healthy. Therefore, if we don't want to change, we cannot use our age, height, gender or weight as an excuse. We'll have to figure something else out.

Still, when they showed her pictures of junk food, the old brain connections lit up a little, illustrating that even when they are dormant, they still exist. Perhaps the brain wants to keep a memory of the way things were. As far as the brain is concerned, if that lifestyle worked for Lisa in the past, it may work for her again in the future.

This is good news for people who have been overweight all their lives, who were raised believing that they were stupid or weak, or who had unfortunate circumstances that reinforced a negative belief about themselves. We are not stuck for life with the neural connections we created as a child. We can actually change them and make our brain look completely different than the brain we have right now.

The ability to change our brain connections is called neuroplasticity. It has replaced the formerly held belief that the brain is a physiologically static organ.

Personal story

This story shows how we can weaken pathways that we've used all of our lives.

I lived in Mexico for the first 30 years of my life. Even though I went to a bilingual school, I found that it was extremely difficult for me to learn English. When I finished my senior year of high school, I was sick and tired of struggling, so I decided to take one year off and go to Canada as an exchange student. I chose a tiny 600-person town in Saskatchewan, to make sure there was no one to speak Spanish with. I moved there in August, just in time to start school.

I lived with an English-only speaking family and I went to an English-only school. It was really sink or swim, because I couldn't master the art of being silent and I wanted to communicate. It took me a lot of practice (*repetition*), but by December I was surprisingly fluent. (Not accent-free, but fluent.) At some point I was even able to think and even dream in English! I thought it was nice to have bilingual dreams. Day and night, through repetition, all of my English neural pathways were constantly reinforced, while the Spanish ones were becoming weaker, even though Spanish was my native language. Back then there was no internet, and long distance calls were expensive (yes, I am *that* young). I spoke to my family only once every two weeks.

As time passed, I found it slightly more difficult to talk to my parents in Spanish because I was starting to forget random words. I would have to pause and think because an English word popped into my head.

When I came back to Mexico, it took me almost a month to be fluent in Spanish again. Then I started college in a Spanish-only university, and lived in a Spanish-only family (mine). Therefore my Spanish speaking neurons were being reinforced and the English ones were becoming dormant.

Interesting fact: *Many children in Mexico stay in their parents' home until they get married. College is just an extension of* *high school, and if the college you attend 15 is blocks away from your parents' house, and if that house also has housekeeping service 6 days a week and home-made meals three times a day, the thought of moving out doesn't even occur to you.*

Many years later, in 2001, I moved to California with my first husband and two boys. Ivan was 2 and Fernando was 6 months old. It was a little confusing to talk to my husband and children in Spanish, and to the rest of the world in English. It was as if my mind was asking me to choose between the two. I couldn't do so because I needed both languages, and eventually through practice (*repetition*), my mind learned to switch between Spanish and English easily.

Your neurons are actually nice and they want to accommodate your needs (not your wants). If you are in a situation that requires that you learn a new skill, with practice you will master it—like me, speaking English only in Canada and speaking Spanish only in Mexico, and switching back and forth between the two languages in California.

How can this information be useful?

When you realize the difference between the conscious and the subconscious minds, you will understand that if you haven't been able to accomplish your goals, it's not because you are weak or lazy, but because the subconscious mind is conditioned to keep you alive, not happy.

When you learn that a belief system is created through repetition or shock, you will also know that it can be changed by repetition or shock. That's the way to accomplish your goals because you are making the *I am* your ally instead of your enemy.

Also remember and be happy about the plasticity of the brain, because it doesn't matter what kind of messy traffic jam you have up there, it can be fixed.

TWO WAYS TO BREAK AN EGG

THROUGH REPETITION   THROUGH SHOCK

There are other situations that will change through either repetition or shock, but for the purpose of this book I will only focus on the belief system.

Chapter 2

Understanding Your Radar

"I am not absentminded. It is the presence of mind that makes me unaware of everything else."
G.K. Chesterton

Let's start by defining the Reticular Activating System, or RAS:

> *"The reticular activating system (RAS), or extra-thalamic control modulatory system, is a set of connected nuclei in the brains of vertebrates that is responsible for regulating arousal and sleep-wake transitions. As its name implies, its most influential component is the reticular formation. It is a set of interconnected nuclei that are located throughout the brainstem. The reticular formation is not anatomically well defined because it includes neurons located in diverse parts of the brain. The neurons of the reticular formation all play a crucial role in maintaining behavioral arousal and consciousness. The functions of the reticular formation are modulatory and premotor. The modulatory functions are primarily found in the rostral sector of the reticular formation and the premotor functions are localized in the neurons in more caudal regions."*

Wikipedia

Please don't be intimidated by this definition, don't even try to understand it, I don't understand it myself. I just thought it was my moral obligation to offer you a scientific explanation. Simply realize that the RAS has many functions, but for the purpose of this book we will focus on something called habituation. Habituation is a process in which the brain learns to ignore repetitive, meaningless stimuli while remaining sensitive to more relevant information. A good example of this is when a person can sleep through loud traffic in a large city, but is awakened promptly by the sound of an alarm or a crying baby. [2] [3]

We receive stimuli and information all the time, such as our digestion, the blinking of our eyes, the temperature of our body, background noises, our breathing, the clothes touching our skin, our shoes, gravity, our feet, the floor, the saliva we produce in our mouth when we are eating, the person who is looking at us and the one who is talking to us, the cool breeze on our cheeks, that slight cramp we just felt ... all of these are among the stimuli we take in constantly.

In a nutshell, we are continuously exposed to millions of pieces of information per second. Since there is a lot going on and we cannot assimilate everything, we pay the most attention to information relevant to our survival. The insignificant information will be deleted.

If you were able to pay attention to absolutely everything that is happening in your environment, you would experience an information overload that would trigger the greatest anxiety attack ever (fight-or-flight response). When given too much information, your mind would not know what to do. Therefore, it will do what it does best: help you survive. It is similar to when you have too many programs running on your computer and it crashes, or when you put a lot of solids in your blender and it stops. We can only process between 16 and 50 bits of information per second and, as a safety mechanism, we disregard the rest.

[2] Saladin, Kenneth S. *Anatomy & Physiology the Unity of Form and Function*. Dubuque: McGraw-Hill, 2009.
[3] *http://biology.about.com/library/organs/brain/blreticular.htm*

Monkey Business Illusion

Please go to YouTube and search for the Monkey Business Illusion video. After you've watched it, continue to the next paragraph.

The video shows some students—half of them wearing white and the other half wearing black. The idea of this study is to count how many times the white team passes a ball among themselves.

Suddenly, while you are counting, a gorilla walks on the scene, looks at the audience, pounds his chest and then walks away. Many people—myself included—who are concentrating on counting the passes end up missing the gorilla. Then someone mentions it and they cannot believe it until they watch the video again.

"Oh my gosh! How dumb! I missed that!" —they think— (and by the way, they are not dumb). What happens is that they are wired to pay attention to what's meaningful and disregard what's not. In this case, the ball passing becomes meaningful because you have to count the passes, and it gets a little confusing because the people wearing black are also passing a ball and everybody is moving around. They really have to focus to avoid confusing the two balls.

The same principle applied thousands of years ago. If your eyes were fixated on a predator, you couldn't get distracted by a butterfly or the sunset. You had to keep your eyes on the predator or whatever appeared to be a predator. That's what the RAS does for you. It tunes out irrelevant information so you can function. We cannot function when paying attention to absolutely everything going on around us. Your mind is like a radar designed to focus on what's important for you.

For example, a complaint that I frequently hear from my girlfriends or female clients is this: They change their hair color, put flowers on their head, wear the sexiest mini-skirt on the planet ... and their husbands don't notice! They even ask...

"Honey... haven't you noticed something different today?"

"Yes! And I'm glad you asked, what's going on with that construction that is increasing the traffic? Did you notice that too?"

Then they wonder if their husbands are stupid, blind, or both.

"None of that," I explain. "I'm sure he loves you and if you weren't there to spend the night with him, he'd notice because you are incredibly important to him. But the love he feels for you goes beyond the flowers in your hair or the mini-skirt you're wearing. His neurons are not trained to view your appearance as relevant. Unless, of course, if because he didn't notice your mini-skirt you refuse to feed him dinner, then your appearance will become meaningful because his survival will be compromised. But that would be a different story."

*   *   *

Suppose that a dentist and his fashionable wife go to a party with another couple, a chef and his pregnant wife. They mingle and meet a lot of people there. Each couple has conversations with almost the same people, but when they discuss the party afterwards, it seems as though they attended different parties.

The dentist mainly paid attention to the dental work of each of the people he talked to. His wife didn't notice that one of the guests had obviously bad teeth, but she observed which guests were following the current trends: who was totally outdated, and who was dressed like a slob. She can't believe that her husband didn't notice the woman wearing the bright crocodile boots with feathers on them.

The chef, on the other hand, paid close attention to the food and was able to observe every detail about the quality, freshness, method of cooking and spice usage. His wife had a lovely time chatting with other pregnant women. The chef, the dentist and the fashionable woman didn't notice any pregnant woman.

Even when we consciously pay attention to a few things, our subconscious mind is handling massive amounts of information we may not be aware of.

When our beliefs change, what we perceive in our environment also changes.

Personal anecdote

I remember when my uncle and my cousin read a horror novel called *The Wolfen* by Whitley Strieber. It was about wolves in New York City, killing people and then confusing the police department in New York who believed that there was a serial killer on the run.

This is how it all started. My uncle shared with us that he had read that book and that he couldn't sleep for days because any little sound at night would make him cringe at the thought of a wolf.

Logical brain: zero. Emotional brain: one.

My cousin, a teenager at the time, made fun of his dad for being scared of the big, bad wolf. "I dare you to read it," his dad said.

"OK," said my cousin. And he did.

One evening at a family reunion my uncle and cousin were discussing how scary the book was.

"Oh my gosh," my cousin said. "You have no idea the effect that book has on you! I made fun of my dad, but it was scary as hell!"

They described how the story grabs the reader, and before you know it you are terrified, day and night, by little cracking and squeaking sounds that previously you didn't even notice.

Something happened in their brains. They experienced the repetition of information about the danger of wolves in the city. That was reinforced by the suspense and pent up emotion they felt while reading it (shock). They were creating a new belief system that influenced their reality. That belief system was: "My environment is scary, because there are wolves everywhere." Even when logically they knew none of this was real, they couldn't help being hyper-vigilant of their surroundings for a few days.

When they stopped reading the book and thinking about it, the neural pathways created while they were reading it became weaker and life went back to normal.

The problem with New Year's resolutions

Nadia, a client, feels frustrated because every January the same thing happens:

"This year I will start going to the gym and eating healthier, because I want to lose some weight." But she wonders if she should bother making that resolution again since she's failed to achieve it so many years in a row. "I already know I'll fail, so, why bother?"

She sighs and she says to herself: "I think *I am* just a couch potato and a pig *(I am* statement) who has no discipline regarding food. Such a loser *(I am* statement)."

Are you like her? Have you ever paid attention to the mean stuff you say to yourself when you don't accomplish something that's important to you? Or when you make a mistake? Or when you are in a bad mood? Or when your pants don't fit? Or when it rains, and you accidentally step in a puddle? I encourage you to listen carefully to your inner dialog. You will be surprised to discover how nice, kind, loving, sweet, forgiving and polite you are with others, and how harsh, mean, judgmental, aggressive, rude and vengeful you are towards yourself.

When listening to the nasty things some of my clients say about themselves, I tell them that they really don't need enemies because they have themselves.

They set a goal, fail to accomplish it, try it again, fail again, try again, and fail again. Then they realize it's next to impossible to achieve it.

That's not the worst part. The worst part is that they know that going to the gym is not actually difficult. Working out for 30 minutes is not only unchallenging, but many of them actually *like* doing it, and afterwards they even have a blissful feeling for the rest of the day. They wonder about this strange force that pulls them to the ice cream bin instead. They don't know why that happens.

The *I am* starts with repetition and shock, and it changes depending on the labels that you give yourself. We think that when we call ourselves stupid, fat, loser, lazy, dumb or couch potato nothing happens, but something does happen. Labels like those create *"stupid, fat, loser, lazy, dumb* or *couch potato"* neural pathways, which will in turn will send the memo to your RAS (radar) to make sure you pay more attention to the situations in your environment that will prove those labels right.

Unfortunately, there's more to it. Those negative labels will also lower your self-esteem and make you feel incomplete and broken. Therefore, you will sabotage yourself and that sabotage will reinforce the: "Stupid, loser, lazy, dumb and couch potato" neural pathways. It becomes a never-ending loop that will push you lower and lower. Then you don't know how to get out of it, so you want to rely on your willpower.

I have an acquaintance, Alicia, who's always depressed and desperate because she has no money and she always has bad luck with her employers. "They are very mean to me" she says. I was moving and I asked if she could help me unpack and put things away; I would pay her and I would get the help I needed. A win-win.

The first day she didn't show up because she had a headache. She didn't even call me to let me know. When I called her, she told me why she wasn't able to make it, but that she'd come the following day.

The next day she forgot to fill up the gas tank in her car, and she got stranded on the way. She didn't call me either because her phone had no battery. It wasn't until that evening that I found out what had happened. "Next day, I promise," she said. The next day she cancelled last minute, but at least she called. I realized that she was the most unreliable person on the planet and I understood why she was always broke. That day I called somebody else to help me, that person came right away, despite her busy schedule, and helped me.

Alicia showed up one week later, ready to help me, and was surprised and disappointed to see that I was already done unpacking. She was upset because she really needed the money.

Her "*I am* broke" belief took over because no matter what, she was never able to show up.

Her "My bosses are mean to me" belief became true again because she felt betrayed that I gave the job to somebody else.

*   *   *

It is also important to realize that, if something doesn't work out as planned and we don't know the reasons why, we will create a story or a label to explain the situation. Human beings, for some reason, don't like unanswered questions. We really hate not knowing and unanswered questions will make us look for an answer, label, association or generalization to explain situations that don't fit in any category. We cannot handle uncertainty.

When I was in high school and college I took my grades seriously. The worst thing that a teacher could do was to announce to the class on Friday:

"Ah, by the way, that test that you took on Tuesday ... I have already corrected the exams and half of the class failed. But I forgot to bring the grades with me, so I'll let you know on Monday who failed and who didn't."

Many of us would agonize all weekend not knowing whether we passed the test or not. We would rather have known that we failed than just be left there hanging.

That's why, in many cases, if there's no answer available we'll create a story ... but ... if the story has the words *I am* in it, that story will slowly move to our belief system (through *repetition* or *shock*).

WE DON'T LIKE NOT KNOWING, THEREFORE WE CREATE A STORY

"I don't eat healthy because ... *I'm* not disciplined." (And the stories that we make up usually aren't nice.)

Have you ever said something nice about yourself to explain why you didn't accomplish something?

"I don't eat healthy because ... I love myself so much" No, I didn't think so. (And when the stories we make aren't nice, they will lower our self-esteem.)

Not disciplined = Not good enough as a person. And when our self-esteem is low, we will sabotage our goals even more.

Because *I am* unworthy and undisciplined, I will eat the whole box of cookies.

I will discuss self-esteem later in the book.

THE EXCUSES WE GIVE OURSELVES AND OTHERS, OVER AND OVER, (REPETITION) WILL EVENTUALLY BECOME PART OF OUR 'I AM'

Since you don't know the reason why you can't accomplish a goal, you make up an excuse. "I know why I don't go to the gym even though I know it's good for me. I don't go to the gym because *I am* stupid (if I were smart I'd go), because *I am* lazy (If I were energetic and active I'd go), because *I am* a couch potato (because I'd rather sit around than going to the gym), and a loser (because winners *go to the gym.)*

The real reason why you don't go to the gym is because in your mental files, you have an image of "doing something else." There is a discrepancy between who **you are** and what **you want** to accomplish.

You need to work on the **I am** and on the words that you use to describe yourself. Otherwise, you'll create a nasty label that will, in turn, lower your self-esteem.

Suppose you are out running errands and you run into a friend. The friend tells you that he hasn't seen you at the gym lately.

"Unfortunately, I haven't been going to the gym; I've been lazy. *(I am* statement)"

There you go, there's your story. It makes sense. **You are** lazy and that's why you can't and don't go to the gym.

My beginning as a career consultant

Before I became a hypnotherapist and moved to the US, my business in Mexico was teaching people how to find jobs: crafting a resume, gauging which accomplishments were worth sharing, and interviewing successfully. As I talked to my clients who wanted to change jobs, it became clear to me that their circumstances were surprisingly unique, some of them even bizarre. Back then I didn't know much about neural pathways or the Reticular Activating System so I called those situations "strange coincidences."

Here are nine short real-life stories that show how life gives us what we believe is true instead of what we want. They're similar to Alicia who is broke and finds situations that will prove her belief right.

The employee who is the victim

"Why did you get laid off?" I ask.

"I got fired. I had problems with my boss who was very aggressive."

"And the previous job?"

"I got fired because I also had problems with my boss who was a bully."

"I see." Then I ask, "How many jobs have you left because you had problems with your boss?"

"All of them."

The salesperson who never gets his commissions paid

"What happened in your last job?" I ask.

"I work in sales and they didn't want to pay me my commission, so I told them I was going to talk to an attorney. They ended up paying me, but I was laid off."

"And the previous job?"

"Same thing."

"And the previous one?"

"Same thing. It's very common in the sales world not to get paid your commission fairly, right?" he asked me for reassurance.

"Actually no, it's not common," I told him. "I worked in sales and I never had a problem with my commission."

His belief was, "If you work in sales you will get ripped off, and if you ask for what is due, you will get laid off."

Guys are dangerous and have to be avoided

A young woman, maybe in her twenties, came to see me with her sister. The sister looked confident, but my client looked very troubled. She told me that guys in Mexico were awful, that they were always disrespectful to women. "In addition to being constantly sexually harassed, I've been raped twice. At every job I've worked at, there are men who don't respect me."

The reason her sister came to the appointment was because the abused girl refused to go anywhere by herself. She knew that if she was alone, the first guy she came across would try to take advantage of her.

I get laid off every two years

A client of mine was fired every two years … exactly. Now he was getting close to two years at his current job. He was already starting to look for a new one because he was sure he was going to get laid off.

Female bosses are ogres

This client left his job because his female boss was a slave driver.

"All these women believe they can abuse men," he said.

"And the previous job?"

"Same thing, an awful woman," he said.

"And the previous one?"

"Same thing, a terrible female boss."

"If you always get these nasty women, why don't you pay attention during the job interview and see who are you going to work for?"

"I did that at my two previous jobs. In the first one my boss didn't interview me because she was out of town, I got hired only to discover that she was very mean; in the next job I decided to pay attention and I was happy to see that the guy who was going to be my boss was really nice. I got the offer and then, two weeks later, he left the company. His replacement? The meanest female boss ever."

I need to take a month off each year and then I get laid off

"Why did you leave your job?" I asked yet another client of mine experiencing career problems.

"Because I had to take off for one month when I got hepatitis, and when I returned, nothing was the same, I was not invited to meetings, and at the first opportunity I got laid off."

"What about the previous job?"

"I had to take a month off to take care of my dying father, and when I came back, nothing was the same, I was not invited to meetings and at the first opportunity I got laid off."

"And the previous one?"

"I was in an accident, and I had to be in the hospital for a month, and when I came back …"

"Nothing was the same, you were not invited to meetings, and at the first opportunity you got laid off."

And I was right, of course.

I have terrible luck in my professional life

My client said:

"I was happy in my job, and then another company called me. They told me that they wanted me and I accepted their offer. I quit my job, and when I showed up for the new job, HR told me there had been a change of plans, and because I had not signed a contract, they couldn't do anything for me. I couldn't go back to my previous job because my replacement was already there. I spent more than three years without a job, interviewing without any luck. I finally found a job that I liked as a controller. The CEO, CFO, and COO agreed that I was the best choice for the position. This time I made sure we all signed a contract because I didn't want any nasty surprises, given my bad luck. I signed on a Friday and I was supposed to start working the following Monday. I was very happy and was surprised to finally have a job despite my bad luck. I showed up on Monday to start working for them and guess what happened?"

I was already sitting on the edge of my chair, biting my fingernails and holding a bag of popcorn in my hand. His story was so intriguing. At this point, with a signed contract at hand, I couldn't predict what could have possibly gone wrong.

"What happened?" I asked, eager to hear the rest of his story.

"Well" he said with a sour face, "HR called me in to tell me that they were sorry. They did understand that I had a contract, but the company was in turmoil because that weekend the CEO, CFO and COO died in a car crash going to a convention. They were sad to let me know that they couldn't honor the contract."

Again, he explains, "I have very bad luck with jobs."

Then I discovered that the personal situations people faced were not limited to their jobs but included other areas of their lives as well. I started asking friends and family if they felt that their lives followed a pattern that repeated itself over and over. I also paid attention to my regular interactions and this is what I found:

My friend who gets robbed at least four times a year

She lives in Mexico City and knows that the city is very dangerous. Crime rates are high and she accepts that as a fact. She gets robbed every three months, each time by a man pointing a gun at her.

"Whenever there's traffic and I see a scary looking guy walking in-between the cars, I know that he's there to get me. But that's normal. We live in a very dangerous city."

I know Mexico City is dangerous, but I have never been robbed. I know people who have been robbed once or twice in their lives, but four times a year? Never.

My cousin with bad luck at restaurants

She complains a lot in restaurants. She's the one who gets the hair in the soup, the cold meal, or her order lost in the kitchen. It doesn't matter which restaurant; she will always find something to complain about. The funny part is that these strange things happen only to her.

Last time we went for lunch, her chair broke, making her fall. Now, every time she goes to a restaurant she wonders what will happen to her. My evil side is almost looking forward to the next adventure with her at a restaurant.

How can this information be useful?

When you think that you have bad luck, that your bosses are out to get you, that everything that you eat makes you fat or that you don't have enough discipline to achieve something, your RAS (radar) will be very diligent at putting you in whatever situation you believe is true. Then you will notice little coincidences in your daily interactions demonstrating that indeed, you have bad luck, that your boss is out to get you, that everything you eat makes you fat, that you don't have discipline, that you don't have enough money, that life is a tragedy ... and so on and so forth.

Understand the power of your words. When you say "My boss is out to get me," you are actually creating something in your mind, your heart and your environment.

Why?

In your mind ... you reinforce the neural pathways associated with evil bosses.

In your heart ... you will feel sad and hopeless, which will affect your self-esteem.

In your environment ... life will make sure you end up with mean bosses, from now until the end of time. Therefore, if you want to change unwanted patterns, use your words but in past tense:

My bosses used to be out to get me (but not any more).

Everything that I ate made me gain weight (but not any more).

In the past, I didn't have discipline (but not any more).

That way, you leave the door open for new and better possibilities in your present and future.

Also, realize that when people don't see something that is in front of them—for example your husband looking for the milk in the fridge, or your son looking for the toothbrush on the counter—it doesn't mean they are stupid or absent minded. Please be nice to them. They are deleting so much information that they ended up deleting the milk and the toothbrush.

Chapter 3

Our Mind Doesn't Appreciate Change

"Progress is impossible without change, and those who cannot change their minds cannot change anything"

George Bernard Shaw

I am a mother, a wife, a hypnotherapist, a career consultant, a scone baker, a soap maker, a dog owner, a sister, a daughter, an aunt, a cousin, a friend. Each identity comes with a definition. My definition of myself as a mother was to make sure that my children become better human beings, that they do as they are told when they are told, how they are told. Being a mother also includes wanting them to obey my wishes without me even telling them. That was my definition, identity or label.

A few years ago, I labeled my son Fernando as a high-maintenance child because he loved arguing about everything and never did what he was told. He had to be woken up 20 times before he got out of bed in the morning. Evenings with Fernando weren't much better. I would say, "Fernando, do your homework."

"Okay," he'd respond. Ten minutes later:

"Fernando, have you started your homework yet?"

"No. I'm coming." Ten minutes later:

"FERNANDO! YOUR HOMEWORK!"

"COMING!"

Another ten minutes go by without any homework being touched, and I'm starting to lose it.

"FERNANDO!"

"COMING!"

For him, saying "Coming!" doesn't mean he is actually coming. He is only saying it to buy more time. The same problem occurred with the shower, dinner, brushing his teeth and every other task.

"Take a shower."

"Get out of the shower."

"Sit down for dinner."

"Finish your dinner."

"Brush your teeth."

As days, weeks, and months went by, and as my hair was getting more and more grey, I realized how difficult motherhood was. I felt drained and exhausted. I was mad at him, mad at myself and mad at life. I was such an inept mother and Fernando such a difficult child. My goal was to have Fernando respond to me differently, and to do as he was told without all the arguing. I wanted him to take care of things without being reminded. However, what I wanted was not aligned with the definition I had of a mom:

"Overbearing, controlling, bossy, and exhausted"

My definition of Fernando was: "A difficult little creature."

And I'm sure that his definition of his life was:

"I don't need to worry because Mom will make sure I do what I need to (and it's funny to see her face get all red)."

There was a discrepancy between my definition of "Mom" and the goal I had (the *I am* versus the *I want*).

There was also a discrepancy between my definition of "son," which was: "Difficult child who doesn't do a thing unless he is reminded a million times" and the goal I had for him: "Do as told without arguing about everything," (the **he is** versus the what **I want** for him).

While I was handling my own parenting problem, I had a client whose situation was completely different, but to my surprise, gave me the solution to my problem. Sue (a loving mom, just like me) wanted me to help her eleven-year-old son, Mike with his bedwetting problem. The mom sat on the couch, and the boy sat in my hypnosis chair.

"So, sweetheart, tell me about your bed-wetting problem." I said.

"Yes, I was doing OK for 5 months, but ..."

"Honey," the mother interrupted, "Speak louder so Alba can hear you."

"OK," the boy started again, speaking louder now. "I was doing OK for five months but ..."

"Honey, look Alba in the eye when you are talking to her. You know how rude it is to be looking somewhere else. Would you like it if I was talking to you and I was looking somewhere else? No, you wouldn't, so please darling, look Alba in the eyes."

Now the boy starts talking louder and looking at me in the eyes.

"So ... I was doing OK for five months already, but ..." His mother cut him off again.

"Sweetheart, love, I know how much you enjoy swivel chairs, but can you please keep your feet still? I'm sure you are making Alba crazy with your swinging to the sides."

The mother probably said that because I had a twitch in my eye, and she thought it was the boy who was giving it to me.

"Sue, I forgot to tell you. I usually prefer to work alone with my young clients. If it's OK with Mike, I'd like you to step out and wait outside."

She left and we both sighed with relief. The session continued.

"So Mike, what happened 5 months ago?"

Mike spoke out loud, looked at me in the eyes, didn't swivel the chair, and suddenly looked like a grown-up. He was assertive and charming.

"Nothing. I'll tell you the truth. I noticed one day how distressed my mom was to see that I was growing up. Even though she complains when I wet the bed, I know it gives her a sense of being a good mom, which makes her very happy."

"So, you don't want to stop wetting the bed?"

"No, because it'll make my mom really sad to see that she is losing her baby."

"Then why did she bring you to see me?"

"She feels she's a good mom by taking care of me and my problem, but I notice how sad she gets when she sees me grow older"

Smart kid—so smart that I learned my lesson too. What if my eternal prompting to Fernando gave me the hidden pleasure of knowing that I was such a devoted and loving mom? That thought alone made me want to throw up.

By no means did I want to be labeled a lazy mom. What if Fernando did everything by himself and I had nothing to do? What if my prompting and frustration was indeed part of my definition of being a good mom? What would happen to me if I didn't have anyone to prompt? My client's mother and I had something in common: We were playing the role of the loving, caring mom but that definition included wanting to control every aspect of our boys' lives. It was like we were expecting the boys to give up their brain because *we were their brain.*

No wonder we were exhausted. Were we doing it for them or for us? We truly thought it was for them, but maybe we were wrong. To be completely honest with you, I thought that I didn't like prompting him. It made me mad, it drained me, and it made us fight. The possibility that there was a hidden benefit to all that drama made me sick. But the sad truth is that some part of me had to be loyal to my definition of motherhood. I also had to be loyal to my definition of him: "Devoted mom and difficult child."

I thought for days about how to fix this. I knew that I didn't want to have this kind of relationship with Fernando. Since I needed to teach him to be independent and responsible, I realized that my goal was to act like a police officer instead of a devout mom. Why a police officer? Have you seen that when they give you a ticket, they don't yell, nag, stomp their feet, throw tantrums, threaten, pout or shed tears? They keep their composure from beginning to end.

I had to switch from devoted (hysterical) mom to friendly, firm police officer. I came up with an idea and changed my approach. Every morning I'd make him a list on a sheet of paper:

Wake up

Get dressed

Eat breakfast

Brush your teeth

Fix your hair

Have your backpack ready

Take your lunch to the car with you

Meet me in the car at 8:10 AM

If you finish this by 8:10 you'll be able to watch a show tonight. If you don't you won't.

In the afternoon, I wrote another list:

Do your homework

Read for 20 minutes

Take a shower

Dry your hair

Eat dinner

Brush your teeth

Put on your pajamas

Be ready by 9:00 PM

If you finish this, I will watch videos with you. If you don't, you'll have to write "I'm always ready on time" 30 times.

We started this the next day. That night, I explained that I knew he was a big boy and that he was responsible for obeying the new rules. He could always ask me if he needed help or if he had questions, but otherwise he'd be on his own. It wasn't easy because I had to keep my friendly-police-officer poker face when he yelled: "THAT'S NOT FAIR!" over and over. I knew he was going to test my limits for a couple of days, but I had to follow through with the changes and face the consequences. I was prepared for it.

But there was something I was not prepared for: the sadness I felt when I saw him the next morning with his list, walking around the house and getting ready by himself.

"Sweetie, do you need help?" I asked.

"No mom, I got it," he replied.

Something crashed in my brain. "What do you mean, *you got it*? What am I here for then? Aren't I your loving, devoted mom?" I thought. I felt a knot in my throat like the one I felt when I took him to his first day of preschool, and I saw him waving goodbye to me with his little hand.

That's when I realized that I was doing it for me, not for him. This new approach was challenging my well-defined "mommy" definition.

I had an empty feeling of, "What do I do now that I have no one to boss around? If I'm not this loving mom who is devoted to her children, then who *am I*?" I suffered a small identity crisis and I wanted to call Mike's mom to cry with her, and tell her that I could totally relate and that life was a cruel, hard bitch. I was proud of my son and proud of the police officer method, but the emptiness remained. That's when I decided to get a dog.

Every morning, in order to avoid the itch of being all over him to offer my help, I went to the car and told him that I was going to wait for him there. I read while I waited. When he came to the car in the morning, he had a smile on his face and was beaming with a sense of pride and accomplishment. I was happy too, though some part of me was still slightly sad. When he asked me, in a friendly way "Mom, what are you reading?" I realized that we could now have a decent conversation while driving to school. He sounded more mature than ever, and I realized that I had a new boy with new interests and joy that I still needed to discover. It became such a pleasure to chitchat with him and laugh together, instead of continuing the interminable battle full of hostility. I lost a difficult child and gained a charming and responsible boy in return (most of the time).

Now, for the record: When you change your identity to achieve a goal, it takes time for your subconscious mind to readjust. How long? Approximately three weeks.

Interesting story: *I always wondered why books always said that it took three weeks to change a habit. Why not two and a half weeks? Why not four? I wasn't sure how I could test that, but the test came to me, slapped me in the face and gave me the answer I was looking for.*

Here's what happened: My whole life my hair has been brown, the outer layers that the sun touched were blonde, and the hair hidden in the back of my head was much darker. The fifty shades of brown I had were always a conversation topic for my aunt and grandmother: "Gosh! Why is your hair color so uneven? What have you done to it?"

I had no idea, but knowing that it bugged them gave me a reason to like it even more.

When my hair started turning gray, the brown dye would do the trick, but when my hair got very gray after an intense day of my son's temper tantrums, I realized that the wimpy brown dye was not suitable any more, so I decided to go a little darker. I went to the drugstore to look for a darker color and my sometimes-black-and-white-self took over the decision-making process.

"I'll try black" I thought, and to my surprise there were also shades of black. There was black one, black two, black three, super black, intense black and infuriatingly annoying black. Of course I got the infuriatingly annoying black, took it home and dyed my hair.

The box didn't betray me. It was BLACK with capital letters and one million exclamation marks. Not even tar was as black as my hair. Since I didn't like it I went to a salon and asked them to please fix it and make it brown again.

"Sorry, we can't do that" the lady at the salon said.

"Please tell me that you are joking, please, please, please."

"Sorry, but black dye is so intense that no bleach will lighten it. Besides, you didn't choose your average black ... it will just take some time."

"How long?"

"For your current hair length ... five years."

"FIVE YEARS!" I almost fainted.

I went to various salons to look for a solution but everywhere was the same ... I had to painfully suck it up. Shaving my scalp was another option, but I'm sure my scalp was also black.

The first week with that hair color was pure torture. Every time I ran into a tinted window and I saw my reflection, my automatic reaction would be to scream and swear in all available languages. I avoided looking at myself in the mirror, but mirrors had a way to find me. In addition to that, my friends would greet me with:

"OH MY GOD! What happened to your hair!"

The second week was a little better, I limited myself to cussing only in Spanish ... and by the end of the third week, the emotional reactions ceased. Every time I noticed my reflection, I would simply accept it, without any fighting, arguing or bargaining. That's when I knew that it was three weeks. Eventually I got so used to it that I loved it and I kept that color for five years.

*   *   *

When we label somebody stupid, clumsy, lazy, irresponsible, troublemaker, difficult, etc. without even realizing it, we are changing that person's behavior. And that phenomenon is called a self-fulfilling prophecy.

"Self-fulfilling prophecies are effects in behavioral confirmation effect, in which behavior, influenced by expectations, causes those expectations to come true."

Wikipedia

The Pygmalion Effect is a type of self-fulfilling prophecy in which by thinking something will happen, you unconsciously make it happen through your actions or inaction. This experiment demonstrates the effect.

Lenore Jacobson—the principal of an elementary school in San Francisco in 1963—showed interest in an experiment that Robert Rosenthal, a Harvard psychologist, suggested. The goal of this experiment was to prove the validity of the Pygmalion Effect.

First, all students in Jacobson's elementary school were given an IQ test. After that, the examiner met with the teachers and told them that some of the students were above average in intelligence. The 'brilliant' students were randomly chosen. The researchers wanted to see if the perception of the teacher would have an impact on the students' grades.

At the end of the study, the students were tested with the same IQ test given to them at the beginning. The students who were classified as "above average" showed statistically significant gains over the control group. This led to the conclusion that teacher expectations can influence student achievement.

Rosenthal and Jacobson wrote the following in their 1968 book *Pygmalion in the Classroom*:

> *"The results of the experiment we have described in some detail provide further evidence that one person's expectations of another's behavior may come to serve as a self-fulfilling prophecy. When teachers expected that certain children would show greater intellectual development, those children did show greater intellectual development."* [4]

Another study: when white men can't do math [5]

In this study, the goal was to see if people's abilities could be affected by stereotypes. This case involved nationality bias. They chose Caucasian boys, with long histories of very high math scores, to participate. The researchers told the students that they were going to give them a math test. As simple as that … if they are outstanding in math there shouldn't be a problem right? The problem started when the examiners labeled the students as "bad in math" by saying the following:

"The reason for this math test is to investigate why Asian boys always do much better than anyone else on math tests."

The moment these students were told that they were not as good as their Asian classmates when it comes to math, they conditioned themselves to prove the researchers right. As a result they didn't do as well as they would have were they not first compared to the Asian students.

---

[4] Rosenthal, R., & Jacobson, L. (1968). *Pygmalion in the classroom: Teacher expectation and pupils' intellectual development.* New York: Holt, Rinehart and Winston.

[5] Necessary and Sufficient Factors in Stereotype Threat, Joshua Aronson Journal of Experimental Social Psychology 35 (1999): 29– 46. 158 Asian American female college students

A second math study group [6]

The researchers gathered three groups of Asian women, and each group had to fill out a questionnaire before taking a math test. The stereotypes being examined were as follows:

- Asians are better in math than other nationalities.

- Women have worse math skills than men.

The first questionnaire was focused on their ethnicity and family origin. Their gender was not mentioned. Therefore, it reinforced the belief that, because they are Asian, they are better at math. The second emphasized their gender without mentioning their ethnicity, reinforcing the belief that because they are women, they have poor math skills compared to men. The third group was a control group who filled out a neutral questionnaire that had nothing to do with gender or ethnicity.

The results were not surprising but still interesting; they confirmed the expectations of the stereotypes. Students conditioned to think about being Asian performed better on the test than the control group, and the students that were conditioned to consider their gender did the worst of the three groups.

Making changes

Did you know that with any change you suffer a small identity crisis? What you will feel is discomfort: a feeling that something is not right. Are you aware that due to the identity crisis, you are prone to return to your old bad habits? Change makes a well-known pattern disappear and the absence of a pattern is scary. Why? Because, again, it can compromise our survival.

Imagine life in prehistoric times. You live in a cave with your tribe, everybody has a role to play, men hunt animals for food, and women take care of the young and gather fruits and vegetables. The

---

[6] Asian American female college students: Todd Pittinsky, Margaret Shih, and Nalini Ambady, "Identity Adaptiveness: Affect Across Multiple Identities," Journal of Social Issues 55: 3 (1999): 503– 18

tribe is happily following a pattern, but you have noticed that for the last few months the main threat you all face is a group of tigers roaming the neighborhood just after sunrise. All the men in the tribe wake up early in the morning, gather spears and get ready to scare the tigers away. Every morning, when the tigers are gone, everybody can go about their routine.

But one day, while all the men in the tribe are ready to scare away the tigers, they realize that there aren't any tigers around. Initially, you will think: "That's good news!" But the truth is that now that nobody knows what the tigers' plans are, the rest of the tribe won't be able to keep their routine without being a little aware of their surroundings. What if the tigers show up when nobody is prepared?

So, even when that change appears to be a good one, there is some discomfort and stress associated with it. Our survival depended on predictability and patterns. A lack of predictability and patterns creates stress. When we experience change, one part of our mind is in 'alert mode.' Alert mode creates tension and uses a great amount of brain power. The mind will search for patterns and predictability to save resources.

*   *   *

One part of the primitive brain is called the basal ganglia, which, for many years, scientists didn't understand very well. In the early 1990's MIT researchers began investigating whether the basal ganglia affected our habits[7]. In his book *The Power of Habit* Charles Duhigg describes the following experiment.

The experimenters observed rats and their habits to learn whether the basal ganglia played any role in the creation of habits. They inserted micro-sensors into the heads of some rats in

---

[7] The maze was structured Ann M. Graybiel, "Overview at Habits, Rituals, and the Evaluative Brain," Annual Review of Neuroscience 31 (2008): 359– 87; T. D. Barnes et al.

order to observe brain activity as the rats performed a series of routines. Then, the rats were placed into a T-shaped maze with a piece of chocolate at one end. Each rat was placed behind a little door that opened immediately after a loud click. The moment the rat heard the click, the partition disappeared and the rat would wander through the maze, scratching its walls and following the scent of the chocolate.

The rats' behavior indicated that they were taking a stroll around the maze with no apparent pattern. But the circuits inside their heads showed something different. Their basal ganglia exhibited high amounts of activity because each rat was processing a lot of information as it wandered around.

The scientists repeated the experiment hundreds of times and watched the rats' brain activity change each time. With time, the rats spent less time sniffing and walking around and they rushed through the maze faster and faster. When that happened their mental activity decreased. Why? Because they needed to do less thinking each time they walked around the familiar maze. As each rat learned how to navigate the maze, its mental activity decreased. As the route became more and more automatic, each rat started thinking less and less. It was as though the first few times a rat explored the maze, its brain had to work at full power to make sense of all the new information. But after a few days of running the same route, the rat didn't need to scratch the walls or smell the air any more, and the brain activity associated with scratching and smelling ceased.

Since the rats didn't need to choose which direction to turn, the decision-making centers of their brains went quiet. All it had to do was recall the quickest path to the chocolate. Within a week, even the brain structures related to memory had quieted down.

When we are changing a habit, we need to give up the familiar and deal with unfamiliar situations for a few days. That involves having our basal ganglia be on the lookout and working more than usual until we get used to the new environment. It's the same thing that happens when we are driving to a new place for the first time. We pay attention to the GPS (if any), the streets, the traffic and surroundings. Our basal ganglia is working at full capacity. We don't have the mental energy to listen to the radio or to have a meaningful conversation with the person sitting next to us. After going to the same place for several days *(repetition)* we become used to the streets, traffic and surroundings. Then we can drive that route safely while listening to the radio and having a nice conversation with the person sitting next to us.

Example of why even a change for the better can be uncomfortable

One day I hosted a glamour photo shoot party. The goal of these parties is to get professional pictures taken at a discount because at least 20 people are being photographed. We get wholesale prices for our pictures and everybody wins. I had to gather at least 20 friends who were willing to get a makeover and photos taken by a professional. I thought it would be fun to do something like that with my girlfriends. That day, the crew from the photo company arrived, along with makeup and styling artists who brought a full wardrobe of props to wear for the pictures. We were not allowed to see ourselves while we were being groomed. The makeup artist told us that the makeup would be much heavier than usual because the lights that the photographer uses would 'eat up' much of our makeup.

After they were done with the makeup and hair, the photographer would recommend a sexy top and a bunch of nice accessories from the wardrobe that they brought. Then the photo session and then ... we were able to look at ourselves in the mirror.

It was such a shock to see ourselves looking like that: "It's too much makeup, my eyes look too big, and my lips too dark!" we thought. What we saw in the mirror was an alien. A pretty alien, but it still made us awfully uncomfortable. When I looked at my friends, they looked stunning. However, when they looked at themselves they were shocked. Some of them even used moist towels to wipe the makeup off. Under no circumstance were they going to leave my house looking like that.

One of the roles my friends and I play is the 'average looking Jane.' This definition includes wearing average looking clothes, light makeup, flat shoes, and a ponytail. Our definition of normal is looking good at a rate of 50%. The moment we put on high heels, we automatically feel different and go from 50% to 65%. The moment we straighten our hair in addition to wearing the heels, we go from 65% pretty to 80%. Adding nice makeup takes us to 95%. When we are at 95%, we won't let anyone take things further.

Manicure, pedicure, and fake eyelashes? No, that will make us look 120% pretty and we cannot handle that! We'll just stick to the high heels and straight hair. No makeup. It was too much. We didn't realize that we looked really nice. Our husbands were drooling, they thought we looked like Angelina Jolie, but we felt more like Lady Gaga.

Another reason we don't welcome change is because we are afraid of being excluded

Once upon a time, being excluded from our tribe meant isolation and possibly becoming the meal of wild animals. So, back then, being excluded wasn't an option. But now? (I'll talk more about tribe rejection in chapter 10.)

My client Linh Mai came to see me because she was anxious. She and her husband ran a business and were very wealthy. In the afternoons she came home to cook, and she spent her weekends washing clothes and cleaning the house.

In their culture it is the woman who is in charge of taking care of the household chores and the guy is mainly the breadwinner. In her case they were both breadwinners. But it was impossible to get her husband to help. I told her that she didn't need hypnosis, but instead a housekeeper to help with the chores.

Her definition was "the overworked devoted wife." Getting a maid didn't allow her to play that role. I offered several solutions and each time she gave me an excuse.

"No, I cannot let a stranger in my house."

"I have somebody that I can recommend,"

"No, I don't think she'll do it the way I like it"

"If you teach her she will"

"I will feel lazy if I don't take care of my house by myself."

She could have afforded as many maids as she wished for. Her number one reason was the fear of being excluded from her group for doing something very different. (but she consciously didn't know that … or that she wasn't willing to change her well-known patterns)

What she wanted from me was clear to her, but not to me: Help her work 10 hours a day in her business and then 8 hours a day in her house, feeling happy and energized while looking with adoring eyes at her husband who just sits on the couch with a beer in one hand and a bag of chips in the other, watching the game and belching loudly. I had to remind her that I was a hypnotherapist, not a fairy godmother.

In Mexico people are used to having housekeepers. I don't mean a cleaning service that comes once a week, but someone who lives in your house and takes care of the household chores, the cooking, and even the laundry. Houses and modest apartments usually come with a maid's room. That concept is well-accepted in Mexico and in many Latin American countries but not the in US.

When I moved to the U.S. in 2001, I realized that the concept of having a housekeeper was rejected by my American friends. "It's not what the average person does." They didn't want to go against the norm, so they preferred to whine about the chores instead of hiring someone. (I'm not talking about affordability because that would be a good reason not to hire somebody, but some people I know can very well afford extra help.)

On the other hand, when I lived in Mexico, I had many friends who were American expatriates. They were American employees, working for an American company in Mexico City, but as an expatriate, they get many generous perks in addition to their salaries. Those perks consist of rent and utilities completely paid, tuition to top schools for their children, full-time maid, full-time cook and full-time chauffeur. Sometimes the package even includes a full-time nanny per child.

I witnessed some of my American friends during their first weeks in Mexico City, being completely surprised by the housekeeper, cook and chauffeur concept. They could have said:

"No, I come from a place where we take care of our own household needs by ourselves. Take your money and the helpers away." But nobody did, even when some of them felt uncomfortable at first. Why? Because they were part of a community of expatriates who received the same benefits from their companies. Giving up free housework would have been frowned upon by their new foreign friends. This is because the practice of having a "maid" is socially acceptable in the new group. Your immediate group of family or friends (I'll call it your tribe) also doesn't feel comfortable when you change because the group wants to keep its homeostasis. If you change, the whole group dynamic will change.

"Homeostasis is a relatively stable state of equilibrium or a tendency toward such a state between the different but interdependent elements or groups of elements of an organism, population, or group."

Merriam Webster dictionary

In other words, sometimes your group will sabotage you even though they know that your change is for the better. When one person in the family leaves or changes radically, he forces the family to adjust their behavior to compensate for the change of one of its parts.

We are a piece in a puzzle and if one piece changes, the whole puzzle will try to make the piece switch back to its prior shape because it has an impact on the group dynamics. That's why the group resists the change. However, when they see that change is inevitable, the group will grieve and then it will finally adapt and adjust.

For example, a family has an alcoholic father and an older son who's in charge when the dad's drunk. The son has to switch roles from being the child to being the adult in charge. Therefore, he starts making decisions, helping mom, and taking care of the siblings. He is forced into the new role. The man-of-the-house role dad occupied became empty and somebody had to fill it.

Eventually his father goes to Alcoholics Anonymous and after a few months he becomes sober and becomes the responsible, hard-working dad and leader of the family again. He wants to return to the top of the family hierarchy where he belongs, but that place is occupied by the older son. The son will probably argue that he is the boss and he doesn't take orders from a drunk dad. Since that role cannot be taken by two people, the son needs to come to an agreement with his father about how things are going to be handled. Perhaps the son could decide to leave or he could step down the ladder and become a son again with a sober father.

Any of those things can happen. As the system takes shape again, there will be disagreements among the parts even if the overall goal was something good for everybody, like dad being sober again.

When we play a role in a group, the group gets used to us being in that role. If somebody stops playing their part, the system will try to push things back, go through some discomfort and finally adapt.

The family baby

Consider a grown woman who was the youngest child, with a significant age difference between her and her siblings. Perhaps she was daddy's favorite girl or she was spoiled rotten by her family. Everybody treated her like the baby of the house, almost like a pet. She's used to being addressed as "cutie."

If someone doesn't treat her as a child, she'll feel uncomfortable. As a result, she has childish attitudes and gravitates towards people who talk to her as if she were a baby. The role she has in her mind is "a cute little girl" and with that role comes the behaviors. She will giggle instead of laugh, stick out the tip of her tongue when she smiles, and make cute faces when she is asked a question or wants to ask one. She has a high-pitched voice, gets overly enthusiastic about cute things like puppies or dolls, and has an old-fashioned haircut and old-fashioned clothes. She cries or throws temper tantrums when things don't go her way.

The drawbacks of the "little girl" description are not finding a mature relationship, being patronized by adults around her, and securing jobs that don't let her advance her career. Little girls don't get leadership roles. She can have a goal, such as "I want a nice guy to date," but it won't happen unless she works on the *I am* and adjusts her behavior and patterns. Even if she changes her *I am* into "*I am* a mature woman" the group will subconsciously push her back to what they know, because they probably had a maternal side in their identities. She will gravitate towards friends who like treating others like babies.

The clown

He labels himself the clown and subconsciously tries to make others laugh, even if he makes a fool of himself in the process. He feels comfortable when he makes people laugh. He makes jokes when others are having serious conversations. When he talks, people sometimes roll their eyes. He is not taken seriously by the people he knows, and when he meets a new group, he won't be taken seriously by them either once he starts telling his silly jokes.

However, now he has a goal. He wants to get a promotion at work, but that won't happen unless he changes the "*I am* a clown" role he has given himself. Clowns don't get promotions and can't be trusted in high-level jobs. His goal won't be achieved unless he works on the *I am.* Otherwise he will gravitate to people who like to laugh or people who don't take others too seriously.

The drunk

Have you ever been drunk and acted silly? Then your sober friends become patronizing towards you. You hush them by placing your index finger to your lips. You make a fool of yourself and everybody laughs.

You drink a lot of water and you sober up, but your friends don't know that and they keep treating you like you're a fool. Since you are not drunk any more, your automatic reaction is a little snappy. "Hey! You don't talk to me like that!" They realize you are sober because the moment you change roles; they change their behavior towards you.

The caregiver

I had a client whose definition of being a good person meant taking care of other people's needs. It started when she was not allowed to have a childhood because she needed to take care of her younger siblings. Mom was an alcoholic and dad worked full time. That pattern remained and she gravitated to friends who took advantage of her and to boyfriends who were looking for a mom instead of a partner. Her needs didn't count. She wants to get married but she doesn't take the step because she subconsciously looks for people to take care of and they will be her excuse to not marry. She never considered that she even had needs of her own. All she cared about was looking after others. One day she stops, works on her *I am*, and stops solving other people's problems and moves on. At first she faces pressure from the group to remain like she was. But they will get used to taking care of themselves. She will no longer gravitate towards helpless needy and dependent people.

How can this information be useful?

If you have a strange relationship with somebody and you don't like the dynamics of it, consider that maybe, in part, your definition of what a good (wife, mom, sister, friend, husband, dad, brother, nephew, grandma, mother-in-law, father-in-law, stepdad, etc.) is not aligned with what you really want. For example, if your definition is to be devoted to your grandchildren but you don't like having to babysit them every day because their parents are too busy ... maybe you should change the definition to one that better suits your needs. Yes, there will be a little bit of turmoil, but you have to take care of yourself.

In later chapters, I will give you techniques for dealing with other's expectations if you find them abusive or unfair. Sometimes they are also good people, but changing the pattern challenges the best of us.

Ask me what happened the day that I announced to both my teenage boys that from that day on they were responsible for doing their laundry. They are good kids, but they didn't like it. After the arguing came some adjusting and then they did it.

If you have a pattern in your life that you don't like, remember to remove the words "I want" from your vocabulary and change them to:

I plan to ... starting today

Or,

From now on I am ...

Chapter 4

Negativity Bias and Life's Recipes

"Negativity spreads faster than any Justin Bieber song."
Vanilla Ice

When a client comes to see me who is very hard on himself each time he makes a mistake, I tell him the following story:

Once upon a time, in a land far, far away ... there was a first-grade teacher who asked her students:

"Do any of you know how to cook or bake something?"

A little girl, after raising her hand, said enthusiastically,

"Yes I do. I know how to make toast!"

"Is that so?" the teacher asked, amused. "How do you do it?"

"First, I put a slice of bread in the toaster. Then, I wait until smoke starts coming out of it and the bread gets all black. Finally, I scrape it with a knife over the sink."

The End

While my client is scratching his head, I bombard him with questions.

"What do you think of that story?"

"Mmm. That the girl obviously doesn't know how to make toast."

"Do you think the girl is stupid?"

"No, she's doing what she knows."

"Why do you think she makes the toast that way?"

"Probably because she saw her mom do it like that?"

"And she learned ..."

"Yes"

"And she is very smart because she observed closely and learned from the information she had available at some point. Do you agree?"

"Yes"

"Should we make sure she feels ashamed by calling her an idiot, a loser, etc.?"

"No, I don't think so."

"Then why on earth do you call yourself those nasty names when things don't work for you as planned?"

(Staring at me like a deer caught in the headlights): "Because ... I'm stupid ... I guess."

"No. Because you are very smart."

"Now you are making fun of me."

"Another story is in order then."

Once upon a time, in a faraway land, a child knocked over a glass of milk by accident and his mother, who happened to be in a rush and in a bad mood, scolded him. "Johnny! What's wrong with you? You spilled the milk all over the table and the food. Look at the mess you made! And we are in a hurry! When will you learn not to be so clumsy?" (*I am* statement) In this situation, the mother's scolding doesn't separate the boy from the fact that he knocked the milk over. Therefore, when yelling at him, she is not only condemning the spilled milk but also who he is as a human being. And the boy learns that his mistakes reveal that he is not behaving well.

The End

We learn that lesson very well, and when we become adults, we don't need an authority figure to scold us when we mess up. We can do that ourselves. Fairly well, indeed. We got the training, and since we are intelligent, we become experts on self-harassment.

"Mm that makes sense—my client says—but I'm still not convinced. What if I come from a loving family and my mom was always patient when I made a mistake and she made sure I didn't feel bad about myself?"

"If that's the case, then, another story is in order.

Once upon a time …

"In a far, far away land?" – he interrupts jokingly.

"No, actually this story was in a nearby land"

There is this child, surrounded by his loving family. And when he was little, just like all children on the planet, he squealed with joy when he looked at himself in the mirror and gave the mirror lots of kisses. If he carried a bucket of sand when he was at the beach with his family he'd brag "Look mom! *I'm* so strong!" and the mom would agree. If he painted something and showed it to his dad he'd say: "Look dad! I made this! *I'm* an artist" and his dad would congratulate him, he even would hang his painting on the wall. And the boy—just like you and I did—kept on saying out loud how beautiful, strong, athletic, funny, intelligent, flexible, creative, artistic and charming he was (all of these *I am* statements). Until one day, an adult, in a very kind and loving way, taught him that while it was OK to say those things while he was little … well … he was getting older and saying them out loud, could sound like bragging, and that being humble was a virtue, blah, blah, blah … "

That's when the child realized that the adults in his life never praised themselves out loud. But he also noticed that those loving adults did scold themselves out loud when they were frustrated.

Mom burns the soup and she exclaims … "how dumb!" (*I am*)

Dad gets a speeding ticket and says out loud … "Darn! *I'm* so stupid!"

The teacher spills her coffee on her desk and says … "*I'm* a slob!"

The teenage friend examines her zits in the bathroom mirror and says … "*I'm* disgusting!"

The young uncle in high school got a citation in the mail for all the times he has been late to school and exclaims … "*I'm* so lazy!"

Notice how all of these statements have some *shock* included (being angry) and they are associated with the *I am.* And the child learns that it is OK for people to berate themselves out loud, but that it is not OK to praise. And he does the same, without believing what he's saying at first.

Eventually, through repetition, he starts to believe all those things. Society taught him to criticize himself even though his parents didn't.

I have news for you. You were born feeling wonderful about yourself, you loved yourself so much that you giggled at your reflection on the mirror. The first time your big brother, mom, teacher, classmate or friend called you stupid you didn't believe them. "What? Me? Stupid? ... Yeah right ... they wish ..." But then you heard it again, and again, and again (repetition) ... until you created a neural pathway and you forgot how wonderful you are. If you had low self-esteem as a baby and cared too much about what others thought of you, you would have never screamed your lungs out when you were hungry. Ask your mother, she'll tell you how many times you woke up the whole neighborhood in the wee hours of the night. And you didn't care because back then you knew that your needs and wants were important. But with repetition you forgot, and you learned that the most important thing was to behave well and look good. Fast forward several decades and that screaming little creature is the same professional adult who cannot utter a single word at his company meetings without blushing, shaking or feeling stupid.

*   *   *

About recipes

If we don't get the results we want—a nice piece of toast, for example—we may have the recipe wrong. A wrong recipe doesn't say anything about us as human beings. It only says something about the process we are following.

A WRONG RECIPE DOESN'T SAY ANYTHING ABOUT US AS HUMAN BEINGS. IT ONLY SAYS SOMETHING ABOUT THE PROCESS WE ARE FOLLOWING.

Alba's cookies

I remember when I was 16, I wanted to bake cookies. It was my first time and I was really excited. I looked for a recipe and I started my endeavor. The recipe took:

Shortening, cream of tartar, eggs, baking soda and sugar.

I didn't know any better then, but my grandma, who was watching, knew:

"Alba, your recipe is wrong. All cookies in the world need flour."

"No, Grandma, these cookies are different," and I kept on mixing.

"Alba, every cookie on earth has flour!" (Back then, gluten-free cookies didn't exist—at least not in Mexico.)

"Nope, these are different."

Still my grandma wouldn't leave me alone.

"Alba, for the amount of shortening you are using, you should at least add 3 cups of flour. Please do this for me; add at least one cup or you'll make a mess."

"GRRRR! FINE! now please leave me alone." I agreed to add some flour, and she agreed to step out of the kitchen.

I made my dough balls, placed them on a baking sheet, put them in the oven ... and what I got were the most disgustingly greasy cookies ever. And they tasted like baking soda.

Nobody ate them and I was mad. I had worked all evening to bake cookies that tasted awful, and the kitchen was a mess. I started eating them and beating myself up at the same time. "I can't believe it! I cannot even make cookies. I must be very stupid. If I cannot make cookies, imagine what will happen when I get married and I have to cook something. I'll poison everyone. What a waste; now nobody is going to eat this." And the cherry on the top was the torture of having to hear my grandma say "I told you so."

While thinking those thoughts, I was eating the damned cookies, as a way to punish myself. I ate so much that I made myself sick and I spent all night and the following day vomiting. The worst part is that I really thought that I deserved to be sick for being so stupid.

Was I really that stupid? Or did my recipe simply have a mistake? This negativity can lead to more tragic and long term consequences.

The story of Sophia

She was desperate to have a boyfriend. That was all she cared about, thought about, and dreamed about. However, all her life, she had terrible luck with guys. They always ended up leaving her, cheating on her or treating her poorly.

One day, she told me she finally had a new boyfriend and she was very happy. I asked her to have coffee with me so she could tell me all about it.

"No," she said, "tonight I'm having a romantic dinner with my boyfriend."

"That's fine with me. Let's go tomorrow then."

"No, tomorrow I'm preparing a candlelight dinner for him."

"What about Saturday?" I asked.

"On Saturday we are having a romantic picnic."

After that conversation, I realized two things:

1. That she only had time for her boyfriend, and,

2. That her recipe for keeping a boyfriend happy was doing romantic stuff all the time.

Did that approach work? Apparently not, because he broke up with her in less than two weeks. She was devastated. There went the boyfriend and her self-esteem with it.

I'm sure she wanted to make him feel special and do nice things for him. She had good intentions, just like me and my cookies or the girl with the burnt toast. However, something in her recipe didn't fit what the boyfriend expected from a relationship. She believed in her recipe and followed it precisely. Her disappointment created so much sadness that it triggered a lot of self-hatred. She started starving herself because she thought that her boyfriend broke up with her because she was overweight, even though she wasn't. That situation lasted for at least a decade.

When I share these stories with my clients, they ask me:

"But why is our mind like that? It doesn't make sense."

And that's true, it doesn't; our logical brain gets all confused, but the subconscious mind doesn't have common sense, it only has 'survival sense'.

*   *   *

Negativity bias

Negativity bias means that if the mind is left to its own devices, it will choose to focus on something negative over something positive. Negative and unpleasant events will always make a bigger impact in our brain. That's a survival mechanism. If we overlook an opportunity to become better, we will probably regret it, but our life will stay the same. However, if we overlook a possible danger, our survival can be threatened.

We all know that "bad news" shows have a larger audience than "good news" shows, even talk shows … if their guests are all happy families, the program's ratings will be lower. But if the talk show has guests who cuss, scream and spit on one another, we will sit all morning in front of the TV, without blinking. Negative events and situations are important:

If there is a tornado coming our way, we need to know.

If the police officers in our city go on strike, we need to know.

If the neighborhood water supply is contaminated, we need to know.

If the airplanes of a random airline start crashing, we need to know.

If there's a nuclear power plant leaking radiation in our area, we need to know.

If there is a sex offender living next to the house we are going to buy, we need to know.

We don't need to know if our community won the national prize for the best schools in the country, if the zoo is being remodeled to have nicer and better facilities for the animals, if your best friend won the "teacher of the year award" or if a local Boy Scout saved a dog from drowning. None of these positive news stories have a direct impact on our lives because they don't affect our survival. Knowing them will make us happy, but being happy won't save our lives. And, as a matter of fact, our subconscious mind doesn't give a darn about our happiness.

Our ancestors survived thanks to their negativity bias. They knew that they needed to pay attention to possible dangers to survive. Had they been enjoying the butterflies and watching the sunset instead of paying attention to a possible threat, the human species would have disappeared a long time ago. Besides, studies have shown over and over that a negative event will have a larger impact on our brains than a positive one.

If our boss calls us to his office and praises us for our hard work and also mentions that there's this one little thing that he would like for us to change … there you have it … we will be ruminating about that little piece of criticism over and over.

OUR SUBCONSCIOUS MIND DOESN'T GIVE A DARN ABOUT OUR HAPPINESS

"Ruminating is like a record that's stuck and keeps repeating the same lyrics. It's replaying an argument with a friend in your mind. It's retracing past mistakes. When people ruminate, they over-think or obsess about situations or life events, such as work or relationships. Research has shown that rumination is associated with a variety of negative consequences, including depression, anxiety, post-traumatic stress disorder, binge-drinking and binge-eating."

www.psychcentral.com

The story of my nose

As a child, I was very close to my maternal grandparents. They didn't live in Mexico City like me. They were in a city named Tampico, by the Gulf of Mexico.

Each year, I'd fly there and spend the whole summer with them. My grandpa was always at the ranch and I didn't interact with him as much as with my grandma, except for the weekends, when we would all go to the beach or to the ranch and he'd let me ride his horses. My grandpa was quiet and observant. He'd never say anything to hurt anyone; he always considered his words carefully. Sometimes he'd give me his favorite vinyl record Eydie *Gormé y Los Panchos* and say "Here, put it on the turntable for me please."

I'd open the top of the record player and place the record there. He'd sit on the couch quietly with his peaceful demeanor and a cigarette in his hand. I'd sit next to him combing the hair of my doll, and we'd quietly listen to the music. It was beautiful music, he was a soothing person and those were memorable moments.

My grandma, on the other hand, was very bubbly and passionate to extremes. If she was happy she was funny as hell, if she was sad I'd have to mop the tears off the floor and if she was angry her words were bullets. She and I had fun because she was always planning nice things for us to do—like burying me in the sand at the beach, making me pretty dresses with her sewing machine, preparing my favorite meals, letting me use her makeup and curl my hair like Goldilocks.

She was barely 40 when I was born and she had the energy to take care of me for weeks at a time. My favorite part was to listen to her stories. She had vivid memories of her childhood and she'd mesmerize me with stories about the haciendas her parents owned and about life during the Mexican Revolution. I went to Tampico to visit them every year for many years.

At some point in my life, just like you … I thought I was the cutest thing on earth, and I was pretty happy about it. Until one particular day when my grandma announced we would have company—that was the day everything changed.

"Today, the Lopez family is coming for a visit. They have a girl your age. She´s such a gorgeous little girl, with the nicest features and the cutest little nose you´ve ever seen."

"Oh, do cute little noses make you pretty?" I asked.

"Oh yes," she said.

"Do I have a cute little nose?"

"Oh no, your nose is wide and ugly. Wide noses like yours are low class."

I was so shocked to hear that. That was the rudest thing anyone had ever said to me. I didn't even know what low class meant, but by her tone I imagined it was not something nice either.

"Why would you tell me something like that?"

"Because it is the truth, and the truth is better than living in denial."

Interesting fact: *When an authority figure tells you something nasty, their authority status, whether real or perceived, will add something to what's being said. I will call it 'the shock factor,' that will make the idea go deeper. When your little sibling told you that you were a mean person, you didn't care; you probably almost enjoyed it. But if your mom, teacher or aunt had told you that you were a mean person … ouch! … If the principal of your school had called you in front of the school and told you that you were a mean person: OUCH!*

The impact of the comment will be proportional to three things: the status of the person saying it, the level of trust you have towards them and the amount of embarrassment and shame involved in the process.

That conversation with my grandma created a complex that affected me to the point of wearing a clothespin on my nose every night, hoping that God or the clothespin would miraculously fix it. Of course nothing happened. All the clothespin would do was to leave red marks on my nostrils.

First, I had the shock of my grandma telling me that. And then I had repetition because for years I told myself that my nose was horrible.

Your current beliefs are a combination of the statements you've been told by parents, teachers, or other authority figures. You took them, put them in a file in your mind, and then pulled them out over and over to remind yourself what the authority figures of your childhood have told you.

From that day on, I completely changed my opinion about myself. I instantly went from pretty to hideous, and I treated myself like an ugly girl. My nose made me ashamed. I grew up like that, feeling ugly and believing life should treat me accordingly. I wouldn't be asked to dance at parties. I became incredibly shy and if somebody stared at me I'd automatically think:

"Oh my gosh, they're looking at my nose!"

Did I blow things out of proportion? Absolutely! But isn't that what many of us do?

When I was seventeen, I couldn't take it any more. I decided to get a nose job. Life would never be good for me unless I changed my nose. When I met with the surgeon for the first time, what I said was that I wanted a cute little nose, like the Lopez girl. To my surprise the doctor told me that a "cute little nose" wouldn't look good on my face. But he'd make the perfect nose for me, and, therefore, I'd become pretty again.

We proceeded with the nose job. And for two long weeks I couldn't see it because of the bandages. But during those two weeks something happened. The doctor (authority) told me over and over again (*repetition*) that the nose job had been a huge success. And even though I couldn't yet see it, I repeated to myself over and over that I had a very pretty nose. So I was already happy, without even knowing what my new nose looked like.

When the doctor removed the bandage, all I heard was the doctor's "Ohhhs" and "Ahhhs" before I could see myself in the mirror.

When he removed the bandage ... I ran to the mirror, I wanted to examine my new nose for the first time. I was surprised to see a nose just like the one the doctor described. If he's the doctor (*authority, expert*) he must know better, right? I didn't see the nose I had, but the nose the doctor had wowed with enthusiasm.

The most interesting part was what happened after I returned to my everyday activities. I was happy. I felt pretty. I got a haircut. I dressed better. I wore nicer makeup. I thought that everybody was going to notice my nose, but nobody did. They even said:

"What? What was wrong with your *other* nose?" I

f my nose had been like a cucumber hanging from my face, when the doctor removed the cucumber, everyone would have noticed, but the cucumber was in my head. He barely changed my nose but he fixed my brain and he changed my self-worth. He made me believe I had a pretty nose and, and as a result, I had more confidence which also made the world around me change accordingly.

Remember this: The negativity bias, at some point in our lives, will make us believe that we are broken.

THE NEGATIVITY BIAS, AT SOME POINT IN OUR LIVES, WILL MAKE US BELIEVE THAT WE ARE BROKEN.

I felt broken when my cookies turned out terrible. I felt broken when I was informed that I had an ugly nose and my friend Sophia felt broken without a boyfriend. Bottom line, we believe we are broken because we are not achieving the results we want, but the results have nothing to do with us, they have to do with the recipe we are following.

Here are some stories I've heard about being broken …

Laid off client

Sam lost his job after a major round of layoffs at his company. He had a nice and supportive family. He was healthy, funny, nice and very handsome. He had savings in the bank which allowed him to take as long as he wanted to get a job. He was able to travel and do fun things that he wasn't able to do before. From the outside, you'd think that that it would be nice to be able to take a break like that. But he felt broken and couldn't really enjoy all his blessings. His mind was fixated (*repetition*) on his being laid off. For him it was a major personal and professional failure. His self-esteem was very low and his levels of sadness and self-criticism were very high. He was a loser according to his standards. Even though he logically understood that he had a lot of wonderful things to be grateful for, he still felt down. Way down.

Decision-making client

Josh had a job in which he made a lot of decisions. Many of his decisions turned out well, but he felt broken when he made an incorrect one. Statistically speaking, he was in that job because he made more good decisions than bad, indicating that his skills were actually very profitable for the company. He logically knew that he was one of the best decision makers in his company. He was a project manager who was very good at coordinating people in different projects. He made his decisions based on the available information, and he was aware that he was successful. But he just couldn't help feeling awful if he made a mistake and he would play the "*I am* a failure" song in his mind over and over.

Why? Because as a child, his parents were very hard on him whenever he made a mistake. He remembers this and now it's not his parents any more, it's him.

Some people will feel broken until they find a boyfriend, until they lose weight, until they get a job, until they change jobs, until they retire. The problem with feeling broken is that the "broken concept" becomes part of the *I am,* and that will make our RAS ignore the information demonstrating that we are complete, whole, important, smart and beautiful. Our RAS (radar) looks for information confirming what we believe that we are. And we are wrong, because we are amazing creatures indeed. We are complete, with or without a cucumber nose, with or without a boyfriend, with or without those extra pounds, with or without being laid off.

Even sad teenagers

In my practice I see a lot of teenagers from high schools all over the Silicon Valley. There has never been a teen in my practice who thinks he or she is good enough, academically, physically or personality-wise. One girl looked like a model, the kind of girl who would receive attention for being tall, skinny, having perfect skin and flawless features. I couldn't believe the reason she came to see me:

"I hate myself because *I am* very ugly."

I wasn't able to put two and two together, and I asked her what made her think that way.

A few years ago, her boyfriend broke up with her. She assumed that her looks had driven him away. Every subsequent boyfriend treated her as if she was horrendous and treated her badly. There was consistency between her beliefs and her reality. Obviously her RAS (radar) was doing an amazing job proving her *I am* (the I am she believed was real), right. Then the "*I am* ugly" idea was reinforced by repetition and shock (the sadness that came with it).

If a guy thought she was pretty, she wouldn't even notice him. She'd probably think that he was a clown who was just making fun of her. But having a boyfriend who treated her as this ugly thing suited her just fine because it fit her *I am*, even if the whole process was incredibly painful. For years she sang the "*I am* so ugly" song over and over (repetition) and I sang the "me and my ugly nose" song. My friend Sophia sang the "all the boyfriends dump me" song. In the end, at some level or another, I think all of us are singing the "*I am* broken song" because nobody taught us to feel worthy and lovable. We got the opposite training.

That doesn't help with our self-esteem, does it? Reflect on what your song is, because that song is linked to the *I am,* which is the reason why some areas of your life aren't working as you'd **want** them to.

If you think you are ugly, you will be paying a lot of attention to the cues in your environment that reinforce that idea. Let's say that the clerk at the bank is rude to you, (maybe he was just laid off and those were his last 15 minutes at the bank … we don't know that). He's in a nasty mood, but you assume that it's because you are ugly. "I'm sure if I were pretty he'd be nicer."

We are good at making up stories like these and, to our chagrin, they are tragic stories with lousy themes. Just what we need to feel even worse.

1. *You feel ugly … therefore*

2. *You feel sad … therefore*

3. *You aren't too friendly to others … therefore*

4. *People react to your lack of friendliness … therefore*

5. *Your belief is reinforced … therefore*

6. *Continue to #1*

What Descartes was missing

You've probably heard the following saying from Rene Descartes:

"I think therefore *I am*."

I'd like to add:

"*I am* therefore I deserve."

"I deserve therefore I receive."

Life will give you whatever you believe that "***you are***" because when you are … (stupid, smart, funny, boring, pretty, ugly, charming, plain, etc.) the universe, with your radar's (RAS) help, will prove you right, over and over.

This is how it works

I am very smart, very valuable, worthy and lovable … (assuming someone with a high self-esteem). As a result I feel in my heart that I deserve to be happy and to achieve my goals. I work hard, thus I achieve (receive) my goals.

'*I am* … I deserve … I receive.' Pretty straightforward.

But that's not what we usually do. This is more real:

I am broken, I have failed so many times, *I'm* not good enough, but still I would like (***want***) to get promoted (for example).

Since you don't feel like you deserve to be promoted you will *try* to talk to your boss, but your passion and your conviction will be so low that your boss won't be convinced. He won't promote you, confirming your belief of being broken.

You will *try* to lose weight

You will *try* to stop smoking

You will *try* to go to the gym

You will *try* to … but nothing will actually happen.

Here you have it:

'The *I am* … therefore I deserve … therefore I receive.' In action.

In order to receive something good you will have to deserve it, and you will only deserve it when you have a 'good *I am.*' An *I am* that's not good enough won't let you receive something good.

Interesting fact: *Some people argue with me about this:*

"Alba, that's not true, my cousin was obese, she had a low self-esteem and was sad. One day she went to the doctor and broke the scale (the scale was faulty). That made her feel so mad, desperate and depressed that it became a turning point in her life. Her motivation didn't come from self-love but from self-hatred."

To that, I respond that no matter what caused it, her inner dialog switched from:

I cannot do it … to … "I have to do it, I know I can do it, not doing it is not an option." They say it over and over, they obsess over it. They never say: "I want to do it" or "I'll try to do it." If I meet that cousin at the moment of her revelation and tell her:

"So … you'll try to lose weight?" She'll tell me: "Hell no … I'M GOING TO LOSE THE WEIGHT" There is determination in her new thoughts. Her thoughts aren't wishy-washy any more.

Ego says: "When everything falls into place, I will find peace."

Spirit says: "Once I find peace, everything falls into place."

Why is this? Because if we don't feel good and everything starts to fall into place, we'll break it.

I've seen clients who tell me that they want to work on their self-esteem and on speaking up.

Others want to work on their self-esteem and also their nail biting.

Others on their self-esteem and their binge eating.

Others on their self-esteem and their procrastination problem.

Others on their self-esteem and their drinking problem.

I always start with the self-esteem, because it is directly related to the *I am*.

When we work on self-esteem and it improves, many times we don't need to tackle the speaking up, nail biting, drinking, procrastination, or binge eating (the *I want*) because as we feel better we are better equipped to tackle our goals.

Does it always work that way? We improve our self-esteem and that's it?

That approach works on your *I am* but not on your recipes. No matter how good I feel about myself, if I insist on baking flourless cookies, they will always turn out gross. But if I work on my self-esteem and then I make disgusting cookies, I will spend less time ruminating on how awful a human being *I am* and more time analyzing and researching what happened and how I can make better cookies next time and maybe even feel happy for the lesson learned.

The same pattern exists with my friend who gets her heart broken over and over. If she works on her self-esteem, her suffering will be reduced, and she will spend more time analyzing what went wrong with her boyfriends, reading books about relationships and learning how to be an amazing girlfriend, instead of ruminating about what a loser she is.

Life is a science fair

I went to my son's school science fair. The children described a problem, their hypothesis, their experiment and what they observed. One of the little presenters brought a sweet-and-sour smile to my face. She was a girl, around nine or ten, her experiment involved cupcake preparation and she wanted to discover what would happen to the same recipe of cupcakes if she prepared it ...

> without eggs
>
> without oil
>
> without flour
>
> without sugar etc.

She documented everything and was very proud of her findings. In her science project, the end result of flourless cupcakes was a mushy mess. But she was not feeling bad about herself. She was actually happy about her discovery. Every time I stopped at a stand, I'd listen to the children explain their experiment while beaming about their findings. Some of their results were aligned with what they predicted, other results weren't, but they didn't see them as mistakes, they saw them as feedback.

Wouldn't it be wonderful if we thought of life as a science fair and ourselves as scientists making wonderful discoveries about what works and what doesn't. In the end it's about workability.

IN THE REAL WORLD CHILDREN ARE PUNISHED FOR THEIR MISTAKES. IN A SCIENCE FAIR EVENT THE CHILDREN ARE REWARDED FOR THEIR DISCOVERIES. IN LIFE THEY ARE CALLED MISTAKES, IN A SCIENCE FAIR THOSE 'FAILURES' ARE CALLED 'VALUABLE FEEDBACK'

How can this information be useful?

Realize that **YOU ARE** NOT your mistakes. Your mistakes are feedback, and **you are** an intelligent person who learns from life's feedback. Life is a science fair, and that feedback is different from who you are (**I am**) as a person. Sometimes you will feel upset because you made a mistake, when you don't get the result you want or when you are disappointed. When you are feeling angry, sad or frustrated, your mind will automatically start ruminating negativity because the mind likes coherence:

"I feel terrible, therefore something terrible must have happened." That's when you should stop yourself. You are upset and you keep your mind busy by repeating over and over: "It's OK, I'm upset right now because I wasn't expecting this, but it's OK, life is good, **I'm** grateful for my blessings, etc."

There will be a discrepancy between your feelings and your thoughts for a while, and those discrepancies feel weird, but hang on. It's like disinfecting a wound and putting on a Band Aid. It will hurt for a little while, but then it will heal faster.

Chapter 5

Generalizations

"All generalizations are dangerous, even this one."
Alexandre Dumas

Suppose that the mind is like a neat housekeeper who wants every little item in a room to be in a particular drawer or compartment. Suddenly there's a sock on the floor. Is it clean? Why is the other sock missing? Is it dirty? Why isn't it in the hamper? The housekeeper will feel stressed and won't be able to move on until she decides what to do with the sock, because lack of order means chaos. Finally she decides to throw it in the trash can. Was that the best outcome for the sock? Probably not. But the housekeeper couldn't stand the idea of an isolated sock that didn't belong anywhere.

Our minds are like that. We don't like isolated events that aren't part of a category, and therefore we create a category for them through generalizations.

I explained before that I didn't like it when the teacher said that half of the class failed the test, and she would tell us who failed on Monday. Knowing that we failed was better than being left hanging with a big question mark in our heads. The mind likes to put information in little compartments. That's why we are prone to label, generalize and stereotype, since not knowing where to place an event will create stress.

Generalization is how we answer the question: "What do I do with this new information (or this orphan sock, for that matter)?"

And because we are not sure what to do and we don't like now knowing, we'll make a generalization and we'll cling to it. That will help us predict what course of action to take in similar circumstances in the future.

Here is the pattern we follow when we don't get the results we want:

We have wrong information: the wrong recipe. We missed a step in the learning process; therefore we don't get the result we want. That makes us feel awful because:

a) we failed.

b) we don't know why we failed.

That's a double whammy.

Then we make a generalization to get rid of one whammy (the "I don't know why I failed.")

I burned the cookies ... maybe because *I'm* naturally bad in the kitchen.

I got a C even though I studied ... maybe because *I'm* bad at school.

I cannot lose the extra pounds ... maybe because *I'm* bad at self-discipline.

That conversation I had at the party made me feel inadequate ... maybe I have weak conversation skills. (*I am* statement)

That woman just cut in line in a rude way and I didn't say anything ... maybe *I'm* weak.

My boss wasn't listening to my idea ... maybe because I don't have good ideas. (*I am* statement)

My boyfriend broke up with me ... maybe because *I'm* ugly.

Then we move from explaining an isolated event and creating a generalization (like the above examples) ... to allowing that generalization to become part to our full time *I am*.

I am so bad with ... *that I'm sure I will never be able to...*

I am so bad in the kitchen ... that I'm sure I will never be able to cook anything.

I am so bad at school ... that I'm sure I will never be able to go to college.

I am so bad at self-discipline ... that I'm sure I will never be able to lose weight.

I am so bad at having fun conversations ... that I will never be able to have friends.

I am so weak ... that I'll always be surrounded by bullies.

I don't have good ideas (I am statement = *I'm* not good at coming up with ideas) ... I don't think I will ever get promoted

I am so ugly ... that nobody will ever love me.

With repetition, we will start justifying why we don't try a new recipe, why we don't apply ourselves at school, why we don't lose weight, why we don't seek new friends, why we are surrounded by bullies, why we don't apply for a promotion and why we avoid dating. That repetition will reinforce our new identities. And our RAS (radar) will get the memo and will want to be a good helper. It will then delete all information that is not aligned with the *I am's* presented above. And that's when life will slap us in the face with experiences and events that perfectly fit our beliefs.

Interesting fact: *We are not wired to generalize when something good happens. The reason we generalize when something negative happens is because we need to place it in a compartment to make sure that we take preventive measures. We don't need to take preventive measures when something good happens. The neat maid in our minds doesn't need to dwell on the things that are working: the lamp, the bed and the desk are in their place, the shoes are organized*

in the closet and the books are on the shelf. Dwelling on why things are in their place would be a waste of resources, (in this case, time). To save resources, we don't dwell on the things that are working.

When we can't predict an outcome and don't know how to proceed, we overwork a little organ in our brain called the amygdala. The amygdala is always on the lookout for possible danger. It looks for exceptions to the normal everyday patterns to determine whether we need to take action to protect ourselves. For that reason, the sooner we can generalize from an isolated dangerous event, the faster the amygdala can focus on other things. The amygdala is a part of our primitive brain which actually plays the role of the tiny housekeeper in our minds. It has to choose between: stare at the sock all day … or simply toss it in the trash can.

Driving in Mexico City

Driving in Mexico City is exhausting because it's the living definition of chaos (lack of pattern). While I drive, my amygdala has to be on the lookout for all sorts of hazards: cars running the red lights, pedestrians crossing the street, vendors walking around the cars. Also, out of the blue, a young teen will jump and land on the hood of my car to wash the windshield, hoping to get a tip. Someone knocks on my window asking for money. There is a parade of people marching on both sides of my car, selling balloons, little toys, puppies, makeup kits, dishwashers. Oh, and I almost forgot to mention: motorcyclists racing one another in the midst of traffic. When driving, I also have to pay attention to stray dogs and holes on the road. I am not talking about little holes; I'm talking about moon craters that will destroy the suspension of my car if I don't see them.

After driving the same route for several days, driving in the city becomes more bearable as I can predict some things: where the massive pothole is, which traffic light is not working and when the train blocks which streets.

Disclaimer: I'm not 100% sure if what's on the lookout for new information and danger is the amygdala, the basal ganglia or both. Apparently, from what I read, it's both ... but ... why duplicate the task? Wasn't the mind into saving resources? I'm a hypnotherapist not a neuroscientist; if you know, please tell me.

A note of caution for all the touristy types out there. If you rent a car in Mexico City, please be advised to not stop at stop signs. If you do, the car behind you will hit you and you will be at fault for stopping. Stop signs in Mexico City are just for decoration.

How can this information be useful?

1. We are wired to look for the negative everywhere: our personality, our looks, our behavior and our environment. (negativity bias)

2. After we find it, we look for an explanation. If we don't discover an explanation we make a general statement like: "*We are* stupid, lazy, a loser, broken, ugly, dirty and/or unlucky" (generalization).

3. Then we feel bad because, through repetition or shock, we end up believing the generalization (a new belief).

4. And when we believe it, we subconsciously look for ways to punish ourselves, such as sabotaging our goals, because our RAS (radar) will push us towards situations that support our beliefs. (custom-made situations just for you)

Avoid negative generalizations at all costs! It's as simple as that. If you want to make generalizations, make them nice, positive and uplifting, like:

I am always in the right place at the right time.

Everything I touch turns into gold. (*I am* statement)

My health is amazing. *(I am* statement)

I always have a lot of energy. *(I am* statement)

I am very intelligent, nice, smart, creative, capable, etc.

These statements don't have to 'feel right,' and they won't initially. With repetition they will eventually sink in and feel 'very right.' All you have to do is give them time.

Interesting fact: *To all those neat freaks out there I have the perfect solution to your orphan dirty sock problem. I heard the brilliant idea from Reverend David Bruner in one of his Sunday services: "Create a compartment labeled 'I don't know', and deal with it later."*

Chapter 6

Positive Thinking and Thought Suppression

"We can complain because rose bushes have thorns, or rejoice because thorn bushes have roses."
Abraham Lincoln

Does positive thinking really work? Some self-help books I have recently read have mercilessly mocked the effects of positive thinking by labeling it "New-Age mumbo jumbo." Are they right? Is the cliché "power of positive thinking" really just hokum? Or is positive thought a powerful tool for self-improvement and everything its supporters claim it to be?

Many of the authors who scoff at positive thinking cite an experiment done by Daniel Wegner to support their theory. They say that we cannot get rid of negativity, and if we try, we will obsess over it, making the whole process counterproductive.

Prof. Daniel Wegner was a psychology professor at Trinity College in Connecticut. He did an experiment based on a quote he read in Fyodor Dostoyevsky's essay *Winter Notes on Summer Impressions.*

"Try to pose for yourself this task: not to think of a polar bear, and you will see that the cursed thing will come to mind every minute."[8]

Wegner came up with a test of the nature of thought suppression in which he gathered some volunteers and asked them to sit alone in a room and to avoid thinking about a white bear. Every time a volunteer thought of the bear, they had to ring a bell. He confirmed, with this exercise, that trying to suppress a certain thought makes people obsess over it.

"It seems that many of us are drawn into what seems a simple task, to stop a thought, when we want to stop thinking of something because it is frightening, disgusting, odd, inconvenient, or just annoying. And when we succumb to that initial impulse to stop, the snowballing begins. We try and fail, and try again, and find that the thought is ever more insistent for all our trying. Many studies reveal that suppression may be the starting point for obsession, rather than the other way around. As a result, we end up thinking all too often about the doubts, worries, fears, and alarms that we have tried to erase from mind."[9]

Interestingly enough, I do agree with the thought-suppression model Wegner and Dostoyevsky suggest. The subconscious mind doesn't understand the word "no" well. If my son is out and I haven't heard from him in a few hours, all it takes for me to get worried is the thought that I shouldn't worry.

That's also true with our goals. The doctor tells us to avoid bread for now and all we think about is bread. To avoid sitting down and all we think about is sitting down. To avoid scratching the scab and all we think about is scratching the scab.

[8] Dostoyevsky, F. (1955). *Winter Notes on Summer Impressions*. New York: Criterion Books.

[9] Wegner, D. M. (1989). *White Bears and Other Unwanted Thoughts: Suppression, Obsession, and the Psychology of Mental Control*. New York, N.Y: Viking.

I'm sure everyone reading this has experienced this situation more than once in their lives. Doesn't this mean that the nay-sayers have a point? Yes. They do, but it's inaccurate.

The reason why I respectfully disagree with authors who don't believe in positive thinking, who dismiss it based on the thought-suppression model of Dostoevsky and Wegner, is because life doesn't end there. After thought suppression, there must be thought substitution.

When I see a sign that says "Do **not** put trash here," I see a bunch of trash piled below. But when I see a sign that says, "Thank you for keeping our city clean," the spot is clean because the word 'trash' was not even in the conversation to start with.

Approaching positive thinking from only the thought suppression model isn't correct. You have to reinforce your positive thoughts in as many ways as possible in order to maximize your success. By removing sources of negative thinking and replacing them with things that encourage positive thinking, you reduce the likelihood that you'll be reminded of the things that you don't want to think about.

Therefore: Don't write, talk or even think about the things that you *don't* want to accomplish. Instead focus on what you *do* want to accomplish. If you want your curb to be clean, put up a sign that says, "Thank you for keeping our city clean" instead of "Do NOT put trash here, next to the bushes."

If you want your citizens to be safer while driving don't say, "Do not drink and drive." Instead, you should say "Thank you for being responsible and driving sober. Your safety is our priority." After seeing a sign like that you smile and think, "Yes! *I am* being responsible right now," because you know you are driving sober.

My point is that we should stop wasting our energy on things that we don't want. We need to focus on what we want because the 'No' moments in our lives are a force that pulls us backwards. After a 'No' one should always follow up with a 'Yes.' And that is exactly what the books about potty training dogs talk about.

Training Camila

Believe it or not, the processes of potty training a dog and creating new patterns in your brain are surprisingly similar.

Two years ago, after realizing that I couldn't boss Fernando around anymore, I decided to get a dog. I adopted a puppy, a small female Shih Tzu named Camila. This was a new experience for me, because I didn't know much about caring for dogs.

All the information I knew about dogs came from Mexico: "If the dog doesn't behave well, smack it with a roll of newspaper." We had several dogs in our house when I was growing up. I smacked them with newspaper every time I found pee on the floor or a torn curtain. I did that for months until the dogs thought it was a game so they wanted to play *fetch-the-newspaper.* In a nutshell: I didn't know anything about dog training.

I was also pessimistic about Camila, because several Shih Tzu owners told me things like: "They are so cute, but so dumb," or "Good luck potty training them." Before I bought Camila, I started reading dog-training books. The books said that it was possible to potty train a dog in less than a month. I wasn't sure I believed that.

I could even train her to ring a bell every time she wanted to go potty, so I could open the back door for her. She couldn't be left alone, since the gate between the back yard and the street was not secure and she could escape.

I brought my little Shih Tzu girl home, and I realized that the dog-training books were right: I couldn't let her roam freely around my house. She'd end up eating dead flies, peeing on the couch or chewing the curtains. At this early stage, she needed to be kept either on a leash tied to my belt or in her crate. Therefore, when I was home, she was on a leash following me everywhere I went. I also attached a bell to the handle of the back door, at the level of her paw.

Every time I took her out to pee, I'd follow this ritual. First, I'd take her to the back door, grab her little paw and make her ring the bell while saying "good girl!" and giving her a treat. Then I'd open the door and give her a treat right after she pees with a good round of enthusiastic "good job" belly rubs, hugs and kisses (and a treat). I would repeat these steps several times a day.

It was also important to keep her from going potty inside the house. I had to pay close attention to her when she was with me, so when she got into the pee position, I had to startle her with a loud noise (like clapping my hands or slapping my palm on the table.) She would stop and give me a puzzled look, and I'd immediately take her through the potty ritual.

This continued for a few weeks. By paying close attention to her and repeating the same process over and over *(repetition)*, she started to connect the dots and create new neural pathways. I rigorously maintained this pattern, constantly stopping her when she was getting ready to go in the wrong place, (the NO command) and taking her out (the YES command) whenever I thought nature was going to call.

I can't say I actually believed in the process; I just did what the book said to do. I trusted the book because it specifically said that I didn't have to believe in my dog, and that it didn't matter how dumb or old the dog was.

Interesting fact: *Sometimes I get overly enthusiastic clients who tell me that they think hypnosis will help them with their problem because they believe in hypnosis. I find that comment nice and well-intentioned, but I explain to them that hypnosis is similar to potty training a dog, in which neither the dog nor the owner have to believe in the process. All they have to do is follow the steps to create new neural pathways. Neural pathways are constantly created, with or without hypnosis. I say the same thing to the people who tell me that they don't believe in hypnosis: that I didn't believe in the potty training manual either, I was sure a dog couldn't ring a bell, but I just followed the steps and the young Camila learned really well.*

One day, about a month later, I was in the kitchen and had left Camila unsupervised for a little bit, when I heard what sounded like a bell. I went to see and there was Camila, sitting next to the bell. I opened the door and, all by herself, she went out and peed, and then she ran back inside to get her treat. She did it! There was the proof of what the book had been saying.

She did great for a few days and I was very happy. Then a few days later, she rang the bell as always. I opened the door and she went out, ran around, came back into the house, and promptly peed in the living room. I was puzzled. I thought she knew better and that I had done my job well. Oh well, little accidents can happen. But then it happened again. And again. And again.

I then did what a lot of people do in similar circumstances: I decided I was stupid and I started beating myself up. Here I was, Madame Hypnotherapist, not even able to train a dog. I completely forgot about what I tell my clients about self-compassion and forgiveness. I followed instead the natural, primitive impulse of banging my head against the wall.

I was harassing myself with thoughts like "*I am* the worst dog trainer in the world" and "I will never accomplish anything with her."

Then I went back to my training book looking for the part that said, "If this hasn't worked for you after three weeks, please give your dog away because you are really stupid."

What I found instead was, "It is normal that after a few days of having your dog do amazingly well, your pet will regress, out of the blue and without any obvious reason. You shouldn't worry. It's not your fault, nor your dog's. These things happen. All you have to do is go back to kindergarten; by that I mean, you must start all over again."

All that thrashing for nothing! That didn't help my self-esteem, did it? I didn't know why she was behaving that way and I didn't know why the training suddenly wasn't working, so I took the road most traveled and beat myself up. (Has this ever happened to you?) I sighed in relief, knowing that at least the author of the book didn't think I was a chronic failure. Then I did what the book advised: I started all over again. In the end, the bell training program worked very well. Soon, Camila started ringing the bell quite often, and I would drop whatever I was doing to open the door for her so she wouldn't have an accident. I'd open the door, she'd go out for a little bit, and then she'd bark to have me open the door again, and then come back, ring the bell, and then bark again, and then come back inside again. It was becoming my full time job to open the door every 15 minutes for the little princess to go pee. I began to wonder if she had bladder problems.

But after watching her while she was outside, I realized that she wasn't ringing the bell because she needed to pee. She wanted to chase squirrels! When she saw a squirrel outside, she'd ring the bell like a maniac. Afterwards, she'd come back inside the house, until she saw another squirrel a few moments later.

The book didn't say what to do when the dog has trained the owner, and that goes beyond the scope of my knowledge. I just removed the bell, re-fenced the backyard, and got a nice doggy door that allowed her to go in and out as she pleased.

Thought suppression and substitution

The book said that I had to supervise her closely for a few weeks, so I paid close attention to her, allowing me to pinpoint unwanted behaviors immediately. When that happened, I startled her, so she'd stop. This was behavior suppression.

Then, I'd show her the new pattern that I wanted her to follow. This was behavior substitution. Even when I didn't believe in the process, I just did it because the book said so. Then, one day she surprised me! It worked! With practice she had created new mental patterns!

The problem with the white bear experiment is that it ends in 'No,' but 'No' won't get you to the results you want. I can envision myself scolding my little puppy with "No, no, no!", but if I hadn't taught her where she *could* go, and how to get there, the poor thing's bladder would have exploded in the wrong place. If you want a good result, then after you deliver a 'No' to something or someone—whether it's your dog, your spouse, your toddler, or yourself—you have to follow it with a 'Yes.'

Interesting fact: *I'm sure you have seen a mom at the grocery story with a toddler in her cart. Have you noticed that sometimes the toddler is misbehaving and all you can hear is the mom saying:*

> *Don't lick the cart handle!*
>
> *Don't toss the eggs on the floor!*
>
> *Don't pull my hair!*
>
> *Shish! Don't cry!*
>
> *Now you know why the little guy doesn't listen.*

Train your mind like a dog

For three weeks, I had to pay close attention to Camila and look for cues of unwanted behavior, stop them, and redirect her to the behavior I wanted.

Those three weeks felt like a year, but afterwards, I realized I had actually made a lot of progress.

We all have a little voice inside our heads that never stops talking; it's there, it's your inner dialog. Thinking that we can let it say anything it wants is like thinking we can let a puppy go unsupervised anywhere it wants in our house: It will make a mess. That little voice of ours, if left unsupervised, will engage in negativity, judgment, self-harassment, generalizations, and overall pessimism, which will in return lower our self-esteem, change our *I am* and, sabotage us. The training we need to give our little voice is exactly the same training we give a dog. If a Shih-Tzu puppy can learn to ring a bell, we all can learn to tame that nasty inner dialog and make it as nice as we wish.

THAT LITTLE VOICE OF OURS, IF LEFT UNSUPERVISED, WILL ENGAGE IN NEGATIVITY, JUDGEMENT, SELF-HARASSMENT, GENERALIZATIONS AND OVERALL PESSIMISM.

How can this information be useful?

For three weeks, make a conscious effort to pay attention to what your inner dialog is saying. When you find an unwanted behavior, such as calling yourself "stupid" after something you did, mentally stop yourself, and then switch to the desired thought pattern.

First notice that you are calling yourself "stupid."

Then stop yourself (thought suppression): "Hey! I am not stupid, I simply made a mistake."

Then switch to the desired thought process (thought substitution): "*I am* actually very smart and I love myself very much."

But what if a few days later, you forget and resume the negativity? Don't worry! Just do what the book says: Go to kindergarten and start over from the beginning. We'll go into further detail in the next chapter.

Funny fact: If you are interested in watching a video about Camila and the bell, go to YouTube and search for "Camila fighting with the bell." That video was taken before she was trained, but it is so funny to watch her showing the bell who's the boss.

Chapter 7

The Transformation of the *I am*

"Our character is basically a composite of our habits. Because they are consistent, often unconscious patterns, they constantly, daily, express our character."

Stephen Covey

When potty training Camila, the cue was finding her crouched in the ready-to-pee position. At that point, I would startle her to interrupt her, replace the undesired behavior with the result that I wanted, and reward her for performing the desired behavior. When dealing with humans, the same process applies, although humans should limit themselves on the treat front. A happy "Good for you!" mental cheer will do. With my clients, the cue is the start of a negative (nasty, mean, sad or angry) inner dialog. You believed you could think anything you wanted, right? Well, you can't, unless you are OK with being unhappy.

The following are some of the *messes* that my clients have created. In such cases, my response is often the same: I teach them how to deal with their negative thinking when they aren't with me. I explain how their negativity makes them suffer, and what they can do to minimize their hostile thoughts on a regular basis. That will start the transformation of the *I am.*

Gustavo

He is a successful businessman from Mexico. He has been married for 25 years and has two children. He runs a successful import company. And when he came to me, he was absolutely miserable. He had become so apprehensive about money that, even though he had more than enough, his financial concerns were a source of pain in his life. Despite having a lovely wife, nice children, and a stable business, he let pessimism dominate his thoughts. He believed that being pessimistic helped him succeed. Actually, it would be more accurate to say that he succeeded *despite* his pessimism. Thoughts create emotions, and pessimistic thoughts create a state of sadness and hopelessness, which was how he felt.

His thoughts followed this pattern: "The economy is awful. I have to keep an eye on my money because it is very difficult to make and very easy to spend. There is never enough. I'm afraid I'll lose my fortune. Every time I spend money, I feel as though I'm wasting it. My business could fail any moment. What if my employees steal from me. What if I get kidnapped?" His negativity was even alienating his friends.

His ruminations were spiraling out of control. It's like riding on a swing: when you start swinging it is easy to stop, but as you get higher and higher, you gain momentum and it requires more effort to stop. The moment he finds himself engaging in these negative thought patterns, he has to stop them, right there, on the spot.

I do two things with most of my clients. First, I tell them the story of potty training Camila and then I explain that I can hypnotize them all they want, but if they have negative thoughts during the day, my hypnosis won't have any effect because their negativity will cancel the positive suggestions I'm giving them. So, besides listening to my hypnosis recording at night, they also had to pay attention to the restless (and sometimes hyperactive and judgmental) little voice inside their heads, for at least three weeks.

In Gustavo's case, the moment he starts feeling sorry for himself and ruminating about the economic situation of Mexico, gas prices, the dollar-peso exchange rate, or the latest stupid thing the Mexican president did, he has to make a conscious effort to stop himself and switch gears to something much more positive. His thought process should go something like this:

"Oh Gosh, gas prices are up again! I knew that the economy was awful, but this?" However, when he realizes that he is starting to be negative, he should stop himself: "Stop thinking like that. Gas prices just went up a bit. Is that really such a huge problem? I choose to be happy and grateful. *I am* safe. *I am* healthy. I love my life. I feel great about myself. Money flows, and my situation is great. I have more than enough. I'm proud of myself and I'm great."

WHO WILL YOU LISTEN TO TODAY?

Even though he agreed that those last sentences made him feel better, compared to his usual thought pattern, he was a little reluctant to try them. He thought that, if he let himself be happy, he was going to become lazy and lose his drive, since he wouldn't be worried about anything. I explained that, if he was concerned about losing his drive he could add something like: "When I am happy, my drive to make things happen is stronger than ever."

He tested it for a few weeks and eventually he realized that, in his case, his drive to make things happen didn't depend on his pessimism or unhappiness. Ultimately, he managed to keep his drive and become a happier person at the same time.

Anna

Anna learned at a very young age that being skinny was a top priority for her mom. Her mother looked approvingly at Anna's naturally thin sister and with disdain at Anna, who was more on the plump side. Anna was scolded for eating too much and for eating sweets. She quickly learned that being overweight was not okay and it kept her from feeling happy.

A pattern developed in her mind. That pattern was first created by her mom, and it remained in her mind even after her mother's death. She learned one lesson well: a less-than-perfect body is *not okay*. According to Anna's mother, eating a little too much (even enjoying food) made you a detestable person.

When she came to see me, I told her the potty training story and then explained how it related to her situation.

For Anna, eating one cookie (therefore "overeating") triggered her negativity, and her train of thought was something like this: "You want to lose weight eating like that you ... disgusting pig? It's as simple as skipping the cookie, you will never lose weight because you don't have what it takes. You are a loser."

The trick for this kind of situation is to halt the self-harassment with a statement like this: "Stop it right there Anna! Yes, you ate a cookie. So what? It's not the end of the world. Besides, you do have great eating habits and they are getting better and better with time, and I'm proud of you, and I love you."

I advised her to pay close attention to her thoughts for the next three weeks so she could stop the negativity on the spot. After this period, she felt much better about herself. To her surprise, she noticed that she didn't eat as many cookies, and she also noticed that she was happier and in a much better mood.

Tom

Tom grew up in a loving family and had a nice childhood, but his parents tended to scold him harshly for his mistakes. This pattern of a mistake followed by harsh scolding was repeated, over and over (repetition). Eventually, the lesson of "You must not make any mistakes, or you will be scolded" was deeply ingrained into his subconscious mind and was kept alive by an inner voice that never stopped reprimanding him.

In addition, one day at school while playing basketball, he made a terrible mistake that cost his team the game. His teammates hated him and the audience jeered. What made matters worse was when in the depth of his misery, his coach told him, "That mistake makes you feel like a loser, doesn't it?"

As Tom recalls the incident, tears start rolling down the cheeks of this 6'5" man. Every time he makes a mistake, he starts this inner dialog: "You knew better than that, dammit! That was absolutely embarrassing! You made a fool of yourself in front of the investors, and the only reason they still want to invest in your idea is probably because you looked so pathetic that they just felt sorry for you."

I went through the same process with Tom and explained the potty training method. From then on, whenever he made a mistake and the harassment was about to start, Tom would deliberately change the direction of his inner dialog. "Stop it! I didn't make a fool of myself. Maybe I was just a tiny bit clumsy with the investors, but they are smart people who see the big picture. I am flattered that they accepted my proposal. I am proud of who I am and I love myself." Even shorter comments like, "Am I awesome or what?" or "I can see why the investors believe in me; I have made them make a lot of money" will reinforce the positive image of his abilities.

Robert

Robert's parents believed in the saying, "Children should be seen and not heard." He was raised to listen to the adults but not to talk. Now he is an adult surrounded by adults.

As a result, he had a difficult time stating his opinion in meetings and when he is able to manage to speak out loud, he'll be very nervous. To make matters worse, if somebody disagreed with him, it would set off a mental litany of, "You are so stupid. Why did you have to open your big, fat mouth? Nobody agreed with your idea. Now they probably think you are stupid."

Just like the rest, he had to pay attention to that little voice, and when the negativity started he had to halt it.

"Stop it right there! My opinion is valuable and I appreciate that the team encourages us to express ourselves." Then the extra self-confidence boost: "My opinions are amazing and everybody, including myself, likes the way I speak up. I'm proud of myself and I love myself very much."

Mary

She was in a relationship with a very nice guy: Matthew. He is handsome, successful, funny and loving. He loves her dearly, but she has this insecurity that makes her think that he is too good for her. Sometimes on Friday nights he has to work late and he cannot see her. That triggers the "He *always* (generalization) has better things to do than be with me. I know that he is out of my league–big time. I don't know why he even bothers going out with me."(he=God, me=trash)

She began making a conscious effort to avoid such negative and self-destructive thoughts. Now she stops that inner voice by saying, "Hey there! Stop that this very moment! Matthew has a lot of work today, but we make a great couple. He's a good catch, but *I am* a great catch myself. I'll give him his space and I'll go to the gym instead. He loves me, and I love myself too."

Jonathan

He is a sophomore in a local high school. He was obsessed with his grades and thought that one C would ruin his life forever: a good university would never want him. He feared that, if he couldn't make it to a good college, he would never get a good job and would be miserable for the rest of his life. For him, all the negativity would start with a C on his report card. "Another C! I will never get into college. I am so stupid. No school will want me. I will be a loser for the rest of my life." With a little bit of training, he learned how to redirect his apocalyptic thoughts to something more balanced. "I got another C. I am smart and hardworking. I will work harder next time. The C doesn't define me, and I know there is a great college and a great job waiting for me."

Julian

Julian, a very successful and extremely good looking software engineer, used to constantly call himself a screw up. He was a math genius with a Ph.D. from Harvard, but his social development was a little behind his peers. He would call himself a "screw up" every time the topic of his social skills came up in a conversation.

"You are *not* a screw up. You were just a bit behind socially. It's not a big deal, that doesn't leave a dent in your intelligence, charm, or wit."

Little by little, he realized that he was not supposed to say—or think, for that matter—those words. So he stopped both thinking and saying "screw up" altogether. After a few months, he told me, "You know what? It's been a few months since I called myself a screw up, because I know you would give me a hard time. Now that I think about it, I feel much better about myself."

Impostor Syndrome

I live in Silicon Valley, one of the world's most famous technology development areas. The region is home to prestigious universities like Stanford and U.C. Berkeley. The list of major high-tech companies with headquarters here includes Google, Apple, Facebook, Hewlett-Packard, Intel, Cisco, Oracle, Yahoo, LinkedIn and many more.

There's a high concentration of geniuses in the area. Despite being brilliant, they suffer in silence because they don't believe in themselves and agonize over little mistakes. To make things worse, they are surrounded by the similar brilliant coworkers, which makes them believe that they are not good enough.

The term for this is "Impostor Syndrome," because those who suffer from it feel as though they are living a lie. They believe that they are not good enough to have the job they have, they frequently disregard or discount their own strengths, and they pass off their own achievements as undeserved. One conversation I had with a client went something like this:

"What do you mean you think you are not good enough? You work for Google! And you just got promoted for the second time."

"Yes, that's true," he rationalizes. "But it's all a mistake."

"What do you mean it's a mistake?"

"The day that I got the interview, I was interviewed by a substitute."

"So?"

"So I shouldn't actually be there. When they find out who *I* really *am* they will probably fire me."

It always amazes me how such incredibly smart people can find such a variety of reasons to explain away their successes. Even among people who not only got accepted to prestigious schools, but also earned a scholarship that covered most of their tuition, I hear things like "Yes, but *I am* not as smart as everyone else at Stanford." Or, "Yes, but in order for me to succeed, I have to work twice as hard as everyone else." (*I am* slow)

Why do they say these things about themselves? Because they allow negativity to take over. They go to work every day, and when they are not paying attention to the task at hand, they are paying attention to that voice that keeps telling them that they are not good enough, and that the guy sitting next to them is smarter and more capable than them. And probably the guy sitting next to them is thinking the same thing.

They repeat this pattern of thought so much that they end up believing it. And even when they get promoted or congratulated for a job well done, they can't believe that the whole thing is anything but a major mistake.

This is what I tell them to do:

"In addition to stopping self-harassment and changing your inner dialog into something more positive, you have to make a conscious effort to be your own full-time cheerleader. Think happy thoughts over and over (*repetition*), thoughts that remind you:

How healthy you are.

How many people love you.

How much you love, admire and cherish yourself.

How grateful you are for having a roof over your head and clean water.

How funny, smart, hardworking, creative, charismatic, eloquent, outgoing, confident, flexible, beautiful, funny, and loving you are."

Every feeling is preceded by a thought. There is no way that you can feel happy emotions after a round of self-harassment and harsh criticism, and vice versa.

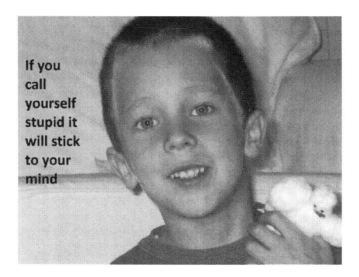

If you call yourself stupid it will stick to your mind

I also sometimes fall into the trap of negativity. However, through effort and repetition, I learned to avoid verbalizing those negative comments out loud. Instead I change my thought patterns automatically. When I find myself saying: "Duh! Look at what you just did, dummy!" I stop myself and reply with: "*I am* not a dummy. *I am* smart and wonderful. I just made a mistake! I'm proud of myself and I love myself."

This habit of stopping yourself will become instinctive with practice, just like brushing your teeth or taking a shower, and it's one of the best gifts you can give yourself.

Train your children to do the same

Throughout my children's early years, every time I heard them say something like "*I am* so stupid!" I'd interrupt them and say, "Never, ever, call yourself stupid, because your mind is very receptive and those kinds of thoughts will stick. Then, you will start doing stupid stuff as a result, which then will feed the feelings of stupidity." That was what I said at first, but after they got the point, all I'd have to say was, "Hey, don't call yourself stupid, because that will stick in your mind. Call yourself smart now."

It became a family habit, and my children learned not to call themselves names. In fact, something funny happened one day when my former mother-in-law came to visit us. After she made a little mistake in the kitchen, she loudly exclaimed, "God! Look at this mess! *I am* sooo stupid." Then, almost by reflex, I blurted out, "Don't call yourself stupid, because that will stick to your mind. Say that you are very smart." No context, nothing. I thought she was going to say something like, "What the heck are you talking about?" But instead she said, "Ahhhh! Now I see where Fernando got this." As it turned out, Fernando (who was four years old at the time) had said, "Grandma, don't call yourself dumb because it will stick to your mind. You have to call yourself smart."

Every time any of your loved ones, especially your children, say the words *I am*, pay attention to what follows next.

EVERY TIME ANY ONE OF YOUR LOVED ONES, ESPECIALLY YOUR CHILDREN SAY THE WORDS 'I AM,' PAY ATTENTION TO WHAT FOLLOWS NEXT

If what's next is something negative or denigrating, even as a joke, stop them and tell them to say the opposite. In this book I have written the words *I am* and *I want* in bold italics so you become extra-aware of them in your daily interactions. You will be surprised how many times people around you say the words: *I am*, followed by something really mean. You will also pay attention to your inner dialog.

When you find yourself saying mean things after the *I am*, please don't get mad. Just change your verbal direction and happy feelings will follow.

Start with yourself and shower yourself with love until you are exhausted.

How can this Information be useful?

Realize that the thoughts passing through your head are random and tend to lean towards the negative side. When you find that little voice saying nasty things, you have to redirect it. It has to be a conscious effort, because we are naturally wired to focus on the flaws, negativity and mistakes. Remember what I said about the negativity bias.

If you learned to walk, to talk, to use silverware, to brush your teeth, to ride a bike and to drive a car, you can also train your little voice to say only nice things about yourself. It will take time, and you will slip up every now and then, but once you train that little voice not to fill you with doubts and guilt, your life will become much more peaceful. You'll wonder how you even managed any other way.

Chapter 8

Gradual Abuse

"The safest road to hell is the gradual one - the gentle slope, soft underfoot, without sudden turnings, without milestones, without signposts."

C. S. Lewis

In their book *Mistakes Were Made (But Not by Me),* authors Carol Tavris and Elliot Aronson make an interesting observation about how our decision-making process can be affected, little by little, by the practice of self-justification. They describe the Milgram Experiment, performed in 1961 by Professor Stanley Milgram of Yale University's psychology department.

The objective of the experiment was to find out about obedience, but the volunteers were told that the goal was to find out if punishment plays a role in the learning process. Milgram gathered volunteers, who were told that they were to administer electric shocks to the participants every time they answered a question incorrectly. The experimenters asked the volunteers to simply administer a small shock to the person, who was hidden in another room and could not be seen. (In reality, they were just pretending and there were no real electric shocks.)

The experimenters offered each volunteer $4.50 (about $35 in today's money) to administer a 15-volt shock to the person in the other room (the actor). They even administered that shock to the participants to demonstrate how mild it was. The volunteers experienced a mild shock and agreed to participate. It seemed harmless, they were being paid a decent sum for little effort, and the study appeared to be interesting.

They went along and the experimenter told them to increase the voltage by another 15 volts every time the participant in the other room got an answer wrong. The helpers were willing to do it because it seemed like a small increase, but as the voltage continued to increase, the participants became progressively more uncomfortable.

The scientist kept telling the volunteers to increase the voltage. The goal was to see how they would react when ordered to give a single, very painful shock as opposed to gradually more intense shocks. When Milgram polled his students and peers about how far they thought the volunteers would go, the general consensus was that fewer than 3 in 100 people would go up to 450 volts. But in the end, when they started increasing the voltage gradually, around two thirds of the participants knowingly administered what they thought were life-threatening electric shocks to the actors, just because the person in charge of the experiment kept telling them to continue.

The experimenters also approached a certain number of people and offered them $20 to participate in a similar scientific experiment. In this second experiment, they said, "I want you to give 500 volts of incredibly painful shock to another person, to help us understand if punishment helps in the learning process." They were requesting a one-time, sudden painful shock. Nobody would do it. Nobody wanted to inflict that kind of pain to another human being even for the sake of science.

This experiment not only studied the nature of obedience to authority, but also examined how the participants found it easier to justify their behavior when it moved *gradually* from one extreme to another.

Here is how "gradually" plays a key role:

"When people are asked in advance how far they imagine they would go, almost no one says they would go to 450. But when they are actually in the situation, two-thirds of them go all the way to the maximum level they believe is dangerous. They do this by justifying each step as they went along: 'This small shock doesn't hurt; 20 isn't much worse than 10; if I've given 20, why not 30?' As they justified each step, they committed themselves further. By the time people were administering what they believed were strong shocks, most found it difficult to justify a sudden decision to quit. Participants who resisted early in the study, questioning the very validity of the procedure, were less likely to become entrapped by it and more likely to walk out. The Milgram experiment shows us how ordinary people can end up doing immoral and harmful things through a chain reaction of behavior and subsequent self-justification." [10]

Originally, Milgram performed his experiments to understand how the Germans could have performed the atrocities they did during the Second World War.

Milgram asked 40 psychiatrists what percentage of people in the US would go to the end; they replied only one percent because that's the percentage of sadistic behavior in the population. But they were wrong, because in the experiment two thirds of the participants went all the way. In addition to this one, Milgran performed more than 16 studies with similar results and it didn't matter if the volunteers were men or women. His results were similar in all of them.

It's important to note that this concept of gradual harm versus sudden harm also applies to situations which seem more normal and everyday. I tend to think of this as the 'gradual effect,' where people continue to participate in gradually worsening situations precisely

[10] Tavris, C., & Aronson, E. (2007). *"Mistakes Were Made (But Not by Me): Why We Justify Foolish Beliefs, Bad Decisions, and Hurtful Acts"*. Orlando, FL: Harcourt.

because the change has been so gradual that people had time to acclimate.

One major example of this situation is domestic violence.

Domestic violence

I will describe domestic violence scenarios in which the man is the aggressor and the woman the victim. However, in my hypnosis practice, I have seen many cases in which the woman harasses the man with violent temper tantrums, manipulation and emotional blackmail. It happens more than you would imagine, as does domestic violence in same-sex relationships.

One TED Talk[11] video that shocked me was one given by Leslie Morgan Steiner about her experience with domestic violence and about how millions of women fall victim to it every year. In her 18 minute presentation, she talked about her ex-husband Connor, who idolized her, wanted to know everything about her and her life, and generally adored her. She was flattered. Who wouldn't be?

Little by little, he started to change—so gradually that there wasn't an alarm telling her: *Walk away from this relationship ASAP!*

When a woman meets a man who beats her up on the first date, she won't go out with him again. Domestic violence doesn't start like this. In many cases, the relationship starts by the guy making the woman feel as though she is her suitor's world, and of course, the woman loves to be adored. It's a magical feeling.

> *"One of the smartest things Connor did, from the very beginning, was to create the illusion that I was the dominant partner in the relationship. He did this especially at the beginning by idolizing me. We started dating, and he loved*

---

[11] If you are curious about TED and want to see Leslie Morgan Steiner's TED Talk, you can find them both on the TED website at ted.com. I highly recommend Leslie's talk and the full TED Talk catalog. TED is a nonprofit devoted to spreading ideas, usually in the form of short, powerful talks.

everything about me: that I was smart, that I'd gone to Harvard, that I was passionate about helping teenage girls, and my job. He wanted to know everything about my family and my childhood and my hopes and dreams. Connor believed in me, as a writer and a woman, in a way that no one else ever had."[12]

When we are treated like dream women or dream men, we love that feeling. Once that happens, we subconsciously start relying on our partners to define our worth. Unfortunately, once we start relying on others to define ourselves, it gives them the ability to undermine and ultimately destroy our sense of self-worth. I've seen this happen before, not only to my clients, but also to those close to me.

I have a friend, one of the smartest and nicest people I know, who started dating a guy. I saw the relationship evolve; at the beginning he was Mr. Charming. She was completely in love. Then, very slowly, things started to deteriorate, and one day she called me because he had beaten her up. When I heard her story, I couldn't help but get incredibly angry; he even convinced her that the beatings were *her* fault for making *him* mad.

I kept begging her to call the police to get the whole thing documented, but she never did. Every time she invited me to her house for a party, I'd tell her that I couldn't go if he was going to be there. I could not be around him and pretend everything was dandy. Just saying hello to him and engaging in small talk as though everything was fine felt wrong to me.

Apparently, the beatings stopped, but the verbal abuse continued. Whenever he got mad, he would insult her and put her down. When I asked her why she didn't leave him, she said that if she added up the good versus the bad, the good is greater since she receives more joy than disappointment from the relationship. As long as she read his cues to determine when he's angry because ... well ...

---

[12] Steiner, L. M. (2012, November). Leslie Morgan Steiner: Why domestic violence victims don't leave [video file]. Retrieved from Ted.com

he's a guy, and we women need to be able to read our guys so *we don't make them mad and create an explosion*.

She is still under the illusion that it's her fault when he verbally attacks her. She wants to be a good, supportive girlfriend to him.

Many of us think "I would never let a situation like this happen to me." But, in many cases, it happens so gradually, we don't even notice.

Tavris and Aronson talk about the pyramid of choice, in which people get more and more deeply involved in bad situations as they gradually progress to worse activities.

> *"When the person at the top of the pyramid is uncertain, when there are benefits and costs of both choices, then he or she will feel a particular urgency to justify the choice made. But by the time the person is at the bottom of the pyramid, ambivalence will have morphed into certainty, and he or she will be miles away from anyone who took a different route. This process blurs the distinction that people like to draw between "us good guys" and "those bad guys."*
>
> *Carol Tavris & Elliot Aronson* [13]

Personal Story

After I divorced my first husband, a good friend and colleague of mine of ten years shared with me that he'd had a crush on me for a long time. In our conversations, he'd put me on a pedestal, making me believe I was the one and only woman for him. Feeling like a dream woman—as he characterized me—made me feel wonderful, indeed. With Edgar I felt important, smart, beautiful, and glamorous. I felt adored, and I loved knowing that someone thought I was all those things and more.

---

[13] Tavris, C., & Aronson, E. (2007). *Mistakes Were Made (But Not by Me): Why We Justify Foolish Beliefs, Bad Decisions, and Hurtful Acts*. Orlando, FL: Harcourt.

A romance began and he loved saying that I was *his* woman. I loved hearing that. I even loved his little jealous fits because he thought that all the guys on the planet had a crush on me.

"A man who *truly* loves *his* woman doesn't let other guys interfere," he said.

Gradually, I moved from being flattered by his jealousy to being mildly annoyed, but I decided to respect his feelings and not let his jealousy bother me. As I saw it, we all have faults, right? And he doesn't see my faults because he thinks I'm perfect. So I could be forgiving. The good parts of being with him were really good, filled with great conversations and romance, but his jealous side crept into the relationship so gradually that I kept making allowances for it.

Eventually he expected me to pick up the phone promptly every time he called. At one point, I even began going to the bathroom with my phone just in case Edgar called.

One day, the phone rang forever and I didn't pick it up because I was talking to my son's orthodontist. He let the phone ring forever, instead of leaving a message. He'd call again and again and again. I finally picked up.

"I am talking to my son's orthodontist. I cannot talk right now."

"Well, if you *really loved me* you'd drop everything for me. I'd drop anything for you. Why can't you do the same?"

I was becoming increasingly annoyed by behavior like this. But, just like my friend, I rationalized it by saying that when we were on good terms he was happy, funny and chatty, and life was a charm. He added something to my life that had never been there before, and with him I felt adored, important, and beautiful. And all relationships have up and downs, right? It's all about compromise. In this way, I continued to make allowances.

We didn't live together and his job made him travel a lot. I remember one day, about 3:00 AM, I started dreaming about a phone ringing. In my dream, nobody was picking up the phone. Suddenly the phone's ringing woke me up and I realized that it was not a dream—the phone had been ringing over and over and over and over. When the answering machine kicked in, the caller would hang up and call again, making the phone start ringing again. I ran to answer it, hoping that he wasn't mad. This is how the conversation went:

"Hello?"

"Who the hell are you with, that you don't answer the phone?"

"I'm home, alone, with the boys. It's 3:00 AM."

"Why didn't you pick up the phone right away? I am here, miserable, missing you like crazy, going insane over not being with you, and there you are, doing God knows what, and you can't pick up the darn phone?"

"I was dreaming, then I realized that it was not a dream, and that the phone was actually ringing. Then I ran to pick it up."

"But it took you forever! What's going on? I had to call you at least ten times."

We chatted for some time, he apologized and confessed that he had a few too many drinks and agreed that he should't have called me at three in the morning. When he calmed down, and after he had finished showering me with words of love, I told him that I didn't appreciate being called repeatedly at 3:00 AM and then being blamed for something that was entirely the product of his imagination.

"Yes," he said. "I understand, but when you love somebody the way I love you, you go crazy sometimes. As a proof of my love to you, I will never, ever, ever, ever call you in the middle of the night again. I promise, as a man of his word, that I will never call you again that late."

"Thank you." We hung up and the problem was solved.

And indeed, he never called at night again.

Of course, in my mind, leaving him was out of the question. "I am fine," I told myself. "I just have to find a way to deal with his temper. He had a lousy childhood. Poor thing." I pictured him as a wounded baby, and I wanted to help him heal. But still, during the day he would call and ask who I was with and yell at me, after which he confessed that he was drunk and that he trusted me. This mostly happened during long-distance calls, since his work kept him traveling so much.

Our relationship went on like this for a few months. One day he was traveling again and I remember telling him to call me when he arrived, to let me know he was safe and sound.

"But I will arrive at midnight," he said.

"It's okay, call me on my cell phone that I'll have on my night table. It doesn't matter that it's midnight."

"I won't call you, because I promised you to never, ever, ever, ever call you in the middle of the night and I'm a man of my word."

"You are kidding me, right?"

"No, I'm dead serious. I won't call you because I made a promise."

That's the moment when I realized something was wrong. That I was with a person who lived his life in black-and-white terms, and that his love was conditional on me following his rules, not about him loving me. If I behaved myself, he was happy. And then I felt worthy, important and lovable. If he was angry, I would cry my lungs out because he would make sure I felt miserable. I allowed him to be the one in charge of defining my worth, which was a major mistake. But it happened so gradually that one thing led to another, and before I knew it, I realized that his opinion of me mattered more than my opinion of myself.

I was feeling sad. I started working on my self-esteem, reading my love letter at night, telling myself that I was important and that I loved myself so much, etc. I needed to feel good about myself and he obviously was not helping. His jealous fits were driving me insane.

My love letter said something like this:

"I, Alba, love myself very very much. *I am* awesome, smart, funny, pretty, creative, kind, and loving. I treat myself kindly because I deserve to be treated in a caring way. When I look at myself in the mirror I smile. It is not just the outside but the inside: my mind, my soul, everything about me is good. *I am* very grateful for who *I am*."

(There is a better example of a *love letter* in chapter 15 for you to use for yourself.)

It doesn't take pages of tear-jerking poems. It can be as simple as this and the key factor is to have it handy to read whenever you remember.

Edgar traveled a lot and that gave me time to think. When you are standing on the outside of a familiar relationship, you start seeing things more clearly than when you are inside. When you're on the inside of a situation like that, it's easy to go with the flow, even when the relationship spells

DYSFUNCTIONAL

in capital letters. It's not until you walk away that you wonder why it took you forever to see all the things that were wrong. So, his trips let me see things from the outside. That's when I understood what happened in domestic-violence situations. Women or men start going down the pyramid, just like Tavris and Aronson explained in their book. At that point it's hard to figure out when enough is enough.

The relationship continued, but I was less enthusiastic and more on my guard. I suspected that things were wrong but I was alone and newly divorced, and the good things were still good. Still, something in my heart had died and that let me see things more clearly.

The last fight we had was about my sons. His business was in Spain, and he wanted me to move to Spain with him. According to my lawyer, I couldn't take my sons to Spain if their dad didn't agree and I didn't even want to move there.

He wanted me to start a major legal battle and accused me of lying. "How can a legal system be so stupid that it won't let children travel with their mother?" he'd say. "Everyone knows that the children belong with their mother. Period. I'm sure you are making this up." He'd also get mad at me and at my incompetence at finding a good attorney. "If that moron cannot help you, FIND SOMEBODY WHO CAN."

Then he started with the silent treatment if things didn't go his way. Or he'd plan to visit me (by plane) and then, the day before, change his mind and say:

"I'm not going, we agreed on something and now you are betraying me. If I don't count I won't go"

"But you already paid for the plane ticket."

"It doesn't matter if I lose the money, which I will" (with blackmail included).

I worked on my self-esteem when he didn't talk to me. In retrospect, that was a good idea. When he called me again, he was expecting me to perform a happy dance for him because he was back. But I didn't. I simply said:

"I'm glad you called because I want to tell you something."

"I'm all ears."

"That I don't want to see you ever, ever, ever, again. That's it between us."

"Are you serious?"

"Dead serious."

And I hung up. Working on my self-esteem paid off.

As it turned out, that was that. I never (ever ever ever ever) picked up his phone calls or answered any of his e-mails. And he did call, 3:00 AM style, letting the phone ring forever. But my mind was made up, and I stuck to my decision.

The distance and working on self-esteem worked for me. I moved on. And I met my husband, Jared, with whom I've been very happy.

Everyone is vulnerable

Whenever I see a pregnant high-school girl, it breaks my heart. These girls are usually not the stereotypical girls who like sleeping around just for fun. If that were the case, they would be careful not to get pregnant. The girls who end up getting pregnant are usually the ones who give in to the pressure and end up having sex to please their boyfriends, because they are so much in love that they'll do anything to maintain the relationship. When they let ownership of their self-esteem pass into their boyfriends' hands, the boyfriend will set the terms of the relationship.

In many ways, teenagers are most vulnerable to the trap of requiring others' validation to measure their self-worth, and they need the most help to form a valuable self-image.

It's important to realize that sometimes we make allowances that can become toxic and harmful. The next chapters will teach you how to take care of yourself and speak up, if needed, to avoid situations that hurt you or drain you emotionally. Don't fall into the fallacy of believing that you will never be abused. If things slowly get worse, then, before you know it, you'll end up in an abusive relationship.

How can this information be useful?

Minor abuses here and there damage our self-esteem. And lower self-esteem triggers more abuse. Over time, the pattern continues and it spirals out of control. It happens so gradually that we barely notice, but, at some point, we find ourselves feeling helpless and depressed and wondering "How on earth did I end up here?" If you work on your self-esteem on a regular basis, then when a little abuse comes your way, you can identify it and stop it, especially when that abuse comes from your own mind.

Chapter 9

Self Esteem as a Workout

"Don't ask yourself what the world needs. Ask yourself what makes you come alive and then go do that. Because what the world needs is people who have come alive."

Howard Thurman

Imagine that self-esteem is like a balloon that can be inflated, deflated, or somewhere in-between. When our self-esteem is high, our balloon is fully inflated, and we feel great about ourselves. When it's deflated, we feel sad and discouraged. We see ourselves as flawed, maybe even broken.

Little put-downs, situations that make us feel bad or ashamed and life's little frustrations will make our balloons lose air.

Compliments, accomplishments and feelings of worthiness will add air to our balloon. A neutral environment with no put-downs and no accomplishments will not keep our balloon (self-esteem) stable. It will also lose air. Why? Because of our natural tendency to generalize and focus on the negatives around us. If we don't work on our self-esteem, it will go down.

Johnny Lingo's Story

Johnny Lingo was a Polynesian trader who wanted to start his own village in Africa, so he approached the tribe's king to get his blessing and advice. The king told him that it would be important that he build many huts, a pen to keep livestock, and farms where he could plant enough grain to support people and animals.

The trader knew this and carefully laid out his plan for a village. He explained that there were other young men who wanted to join him, and he pointed to a site on a nearby hill where he planned to live. The king consented.

"When the time comes, may I purchase one of your daughters to start a family?" Johnny asked. The buying of women was the custom of that African tribe in that place and time, and cattle were the primary means of barter.

The king liked the young man, and was pleased with the offer. "Absolutely," the king responded enthusiastically. "Get your village built, raise some cattle, then come back to see me. I have many daughters, and I will give you a good value for your cattle."

A year passed. The young chieftain arrived at the king's hut with a small herd of cattle, indicating that he was ready to purchase a wife. "Take your pick; all of my daughters are over there, in that special maidens' hut," the king indicated. After a short while, the younger chief returned, bringing with him a young woman who stood in dirty clothes, bent over, and dirty. "This is the woman I want to purchase, Your Highness," said the suitor. "I will offer you nine cows for her."

The king was taken aback. "Are you mad? Of all the daughters I have, this one is the most miserable and disagreeable. She is always frowning and moody; she does not sing nor does she dress well. She is certainly not worth nine cows! Two, three cows at best, but not nine."

"Sire," said the chieftain, "I know what I am doing. I insist on giving you nine cows for her. She will be my queen." Reluctantly, the king accepted the offer, insisting that the younger man deliver the payment in increments of two or three cows at a time. "I do not want anyone to know that I charged you so much for such a miserable bride." The young man made his payment, and took the woman, back to his village.

Several years passed. As was his custom, the king wandered among the villages to see how things were progressing, and to gather knowledge of his people. He came across the same young chieftain's group of huts, and was immediately impressed by the village's prosperity and the upbeat mood there.

He also couldn't help noticing a beautiful woman walking with head held high and smiling broadly. Her warmth and energy was clearly spreading to those around her. "I see you are doing well, son," said the king. "And that woman—she's absolutely beautiful. Who is she? Is that my daughter—the one you paid so much for?"

"I always saw her as worth much more, sire," said the younger man. "And when I treated her like she had greater value, she became a queen. She's my nine-cow wife. She was never anything less, in my eyes."

The moral of the story is that Johnny Lingo treated his wife as a nine-cow woman, and little by little, (repetition), she ended up believing that she was worthy. Johnny was able to help her change her learned inner dialog of "not as good as my sisters," to "you are worthy no matter what."

When I read this story as a teenager, I sat and wondered about how lucky this woman was, and how I would love to find a Johnny Lingo in my life, I fantasized about a Shaun-Cassidy-looking-Johnny Lingo. We all want to be rescued, don't we? But then I wondered: What will happen to me if, after finding my Johnny Lingo, he leaves me for somebody else? If my self-esteem was in his hands because he built it, what would happen to me if he left?

*   *   *

I come from the generation of Mexico City girls from the 1970s during which all the Disney movies were about a beautiful, kind, ready to forgive, slow to speak up princess who ends up being rescued by a wonderful, incredibly good-looking and brave Prince Charming who discovers her, falls in love with her flawless beauty and kindness, rescues her and takes her to his castle to live happily ever after. Warrior princesses? Never! They had to be vulnerable and needed a guy to rescue them. (I'm still waiting for a plus-size princess.)

I remember watching those movies with a bag of popcorn in one hand and a tissue full of tears in the other, weeping and wondering what it would be like if I was as beautiful and as virtuous as Snow White and what kind of prince life would have in store for me.

Then came the comments from some adults in my life

"Stay in the shadow while at the beach—you don't want to get too dark, guys don't like dark women"—back then nobody gave a damn about skin cancer or the ozone layer, the issue was ... to have a guy find you appealing. That was the ultimate prize!

I always tanned beautifully, and I'd get Concha Nacar cream from some adult: "Here, you are way too dark, this cream will make your skin fair again." (Snow White was fair, right? Or was it Cinderella? Or Sleeping Beauty?) They were light skinned and they got a Prince Charming to rescue them. None of them had tans from what I remember. Maybe they also had a relative who bought Concha Nacar for them to look light and pretty.

When I was in high school, I went to visit my grandparents in Tampico (as I did every summer) and my girlfriend invited a bunch of her friends to my grandparents' house and a jerk—yes, a jerk—started talking about how men were anatomically much more intelligent than women.

I was pissed. He was already in college and studying to be an electrical engineer, I was in 10th grade, but still I blurted out:

"I bet I am smarter than you, smart-ass" I said.

"Oh yeah?" he said, "Solve this."

He grabbed a napkin and started drawing arrows and numbers on it and I remember praying in silence: "Oh please God, show me your mercy, let me show this jerk that a woman can be smart, please, please, don't let me make a fool of myself in front of all these people, help me with the mess I just created, he deserves to be humiliated and put down. Please, please, please dear loving God."

He was drawing with his more-than-ever-jerk-face, and I was praying ... He handed me his napkin, and then I realized ...

Those are vectors! Ha! That was amazing! I just learned about vectors at school! And because my dad is a Chemical Engineer, he always helped me with Math, Chemistry and Physics, and I got amazing grades in those subjects. (Thank you God! Thank you, thank you, thank you! And thank you to my dad too.)

Disguising my happy dance and my big fat smile, I proceeded to solve them quickly, and I got them right. Then I wrote a more advanced physics problem for him and handed him the napkin.

"Here, those are vectors, here is the answer, and I have a problem for you" (asshole).

He grabbed the napkin and his face was priceless, and more priceless when he saw that he couldn't solve the problem I gave him. (I couldn't either but I wasn't going to tell him that.)

Everybody was laughing at him, and I enjoyed my glorious moments. Then my grandma called me to have a little chat with me.

"I saw what you just did, and believe me, it was not OK."

"What do you mean it was not OK? Did you hear what the moron said? That guys are smarter than women."

"I saw and heard everything Alba, but a real woman shows submission to her guy."

"Gosh grandma, he's not my guy."

"And after what you just did, he will never be. Your job as a woman is to support your guy, not to rub in his face how stupid he is; you have to pretend you are less smart than him and admire him for his intelligence. If you keep on proving yourself smart, nobody will want to marry you. Be wise and pretend to be stupid."

There went my glorious moment. Feeling shitty and thinking that I knew nothing.

As a teenager I was constantly bombarded by my grandmother telling me that my duty as a woman was to marry well, to support my man and to be a loving mom. Work as a teacher or have a part-time job that let me take care of my kids and husband, and of course, I had to know how to cook. Being a successful professional was absolutely out of the question. What if I have a better job than my guy? No guy will want me then. That was the deal. To get married.

"Spinsters are despised by society. It's better to be miserably married than to be happily single, for your reputation's sake," That's the song I heard over and over.

When I turned seventeen, I switched from a life of "no suitors" to being courted by a bunch of twenty-eight-year-old guys. I don't know why that was, especially when at seventeen I looked eleven. I have always looked much younger. Now I love it, but back then it was like a curse. My twenty-eight-year-old suitors were "good guys" as everybody told me. Done with their studies, handsome, polite, classy and with good jobs.

But ... what did Alba have to say about that?

"No way, twenty-eight? They look more like my dad's friends than mine. Too old, sorry to disappoint everyone."

"You have to be reasonable, you should consider yourself lucky that guys like them fancy you. When you are young, the age difference is noticeable, but as you mature, the gap between your guy and you will be less. Besides, you don't want to be your partner's age, since at some point he will find you old and will want to switch to a younger model."

In a nutshell, I was raised to be a wife and a mother, and I learned that my self-worth was based on the type of guy who wanted to do me the favor of marrying me. Even Walt Disney movies back then presented the image of the submissive, pretty, light-skinned and of course ... super thin princess. None of them were professionals, their virtues were their beauty and their kindness ... and the ultimate prize: a husband.

I cannot blame my grandma, parents, relatives and teachers, because they raised me with much more love than what they received. They did the best they could, just as I do with my children, and at some point in the future, when the educational trends change, I will probably learn about all the things that I did wrong.

It took me forever to realize the valuable information that I will share with you right now:

Nobody is in charge of defining your value, that's your job

No guy is going to rescue you, no boss is going to discover your hidden talents, and you won't win a popularity contest with your peers. It is your job to rescue yourself, to discover your hidden talents and win a popularity contest—with yourself. And ... you are valuable ... just as you are. There aren't Johnny Lingos out there.

My clients are usually kind-hearted people; they mean well and have love in their hearts. When I ask them to take all that kindness and compassion they have for others and make a U-turn, they look at me puzzled.

I cannot do that; I will become arrogant if I do.

I cannot do that; I will become a narcissist.

I cannot do that; it doesn't feel right.

I cannot do that; I was trained to be humble.

The truth is this: if you want to be happy and healthy, if you want to achieve your goals and to have healthy relationships with others:

You cannot afford not to do that!

It's like wanting to be physically fit and refusing to exercise because you think you will become arrogant, narcissist and not-so-humble. If you take care of your body by exercising and eating right, if you take care of your mind by learning and studying, taking care of your heart and emotions is just as natural. All you have do is follow a process that, unfortunately, is not yet taught in schools. But here I present it—on a silver tray for you.

Self-esteem, little exercises

1. Practice monitoring your thoughts

2. Be kind to yourself, no matter what

3. Let yourself feel sad or angry

4. Act as though you trust your opinions

5. Use the nicest items you have

6. Stop over-apologizing

7. Carry yourself like a king or queen

8. Watch what you joke about

9. Practice empathic singing

10. Say thank you when complimented

1. Practice monitoring your thoughts

It only takes three weeks to create a habit.

Remember how I potty trained my dog? I had to keep an eye on her, then she was able to stop herself and go in the right place. If you keep an eye on your thoughts, it will become a habit and you will be able to stop negativity right in its tracks. Refer to chapter 7 for more details. Three weeks of constant attention to your inner dialog will feel like a decade, believe me, but then ... it becomes easier. Sometimes, if things fall apart, you will have to go back to kindergarten, and it's OK.

2. Be kind to yourself, no matter what

The same way cheerleaders cheer their sports team, you will love becoming your own personal cheerleader. When you wake up in the morning and you look at yourself in the mirror say, or at least think, "Oh my God, do I look great today!" or "I love my face, my body!"

If you need ideas about how to do this, go to YouTube and search for "Jessica's daily affirmation." You will see a blonde girl with curly hair standing on the sink of the bathroom. It has more than 15 million hits and you will see why. If we all did what she does ... that would be so awesome.

Disclaimer: You may not want to stand on your bathroom sink. I'm not worried about you, but about the sink.

When part of your body hurts or is ill, talk to it as you would talk to a beloved baby:

"Dear feet, thank you for taking me to a lot of places today. I will put you in warm water and give you a massage later."

"Dear head, I love you so much, I'll lie down for a little bit."

"Dear tummy, I ate a little too much, I apologize, I love you, I will give you nourishing foods from now on."

"Dear cells, I love you and I'm grateful that you take good care of me, I will take care of you too."

"Dear face, I see a tiny wrinkle next to your eye, it's from so much smiling. You are growing wise and happy."

"I see a pimple; I'll take care of it with love."

"My pants don't fit, I probably ate a little too much. It's OK, I know I can do better, still, *I am* not a number. Masterpieces like me cannot be defined by a shallow number."

Aggressive thoughts towards our bodies? NEVER! I must warn you that at first it will feel funny—of course it will feel funny! If you haven't said a nice thing about yourself in the last twenty years, it has to feel funny! Your mind doesn't speak that language. But it will, just give it three weeks to create those shiny, beautiful, loving and happy new neural pathways.

If you are stuck with yourself all your life, doesn't it make sense to at least become your best friend to make the journey more pleasurable?

IF YOU ARE STUCK WITH YOURSELF ALL YOUR LIFE, DOESN'T IT MAKE SENSE TO AT LEAST BECOME YOUR BEST FRIEND TO MAKE THE JOURNEY MORE PLEASURABLE?

People who suffer from alcoholism, chain-smoking or overeating addictions tend to feel guilty after they indulge in their bad habits. But what do they do then? They overeat again to punish themselves. Everything began with the negative statements of:

"I'm not good enough,"

"I'm not important," or, even worse,

"I'm trash."

It becomes a vicious cycle: you overeat and you feel sick to your stomach. You call yourself a pig, and because you are a pig, you overeat again.

1. You overeat ... therefore

2. You feel sick to your stomach ... therefore

3. You get mad at yourself ... therefore

4. You call yourself a disgusting pig (or something similar) ...

   therefore

5. Go to step #1

I like asking my clients something like:

(If he is a guy) "Suppose that you are walking on the street and a group of incredibly good looking women stare at you, what's the first thought that will come to your mind?"

"Oh Gosh! My fly is probably down!"

"From now on switch that thought to this one: ... 'Wow! I'm a tiger!'"

I ask the same question to women ... "If you are walking on the street and a group of male top models stare at you ... what will you think?"

"That they are probably making fun of me."

"Wrong. This is what you have to think: 'Isn't today their lucky day.'"

And my client smiles, giggles and blushes at the same time, thinks for a second and then she asks: "But ... what if nobody looks at me?"

"If that's the case you say: 'So absent minded, they don't know what they are missing!'"

Your body is one of the most wonderful things on the planet, and your body's goal is to let you live a long and happy life. It deserves to be treated with love and care. Your mind is a living miracle. Things that are treated with love will flourish, while things that are mistreated will deteriorate. Shower your body with love, kind words, and loving thoughts. Some people even treat their plants better than they treat themselves.

3. Let yourself feel sad or angry

A client comes back and tells me that he hasn't been doing too well.

"Why is that? Are you having problems listening to your hypnosis recording?" "No, I have been listening to it, but the other day I was angry, very angry, and I know that you tell me to stay positive, so I was angry twice, first for the reason that got me angry, and second, I was angry because I was angry!"

"I never told you not to be angry."

"Well, isn't the whole point of coming to see you to feel good?"

"Yes, but you have to realize that anger, sadness and disappointment are part of life, and the only thing you can control are your thoughts. Your feelings take time to come or go away.

For example, you wake up in the morning and, like many people on this planet, you are in a bad mood. The bad mood can be many things. What if your blood sugar levels are low after fasting for so many hours? What if you are going through hormonal changes, or you are really tired and you simply are in a bad mood? It's like having a triple espresso and expecting to feel peaceful and calm afterwards. You won't because the caffeine needs time to leave your body, and while that happens, you are stuck with the symptoms you are having. The chemicals your body releases, adrenaline for example, follow a process before leaving your body. If you have adrenaline making you mad, and then you decide to be mad because you are mad, that will make your body release more adrenaline. Just allow your feelings to be. When the chemicals leave your body, you will feel better. If you want to do something to help, then drink water and relax.

SOMETIMES WE ARE MAD FOR TWO REASONS. FIRST, FOR THE REASON THAT GOT US MAD IN THE FIRST PLACE. THEN WE GET MAD ABOUT BEING MAD.

When in a good mood we love our car, our job, our family, etc. When in a bad mood, we hate our car, our boss and our family gets on our nerves. We are not objective.

We feel lousy, and that curious mind of ours (who doesn't like question marks) makes us want to know why we feel that way, and since there's no apparent reason we will make one up:

"I feel lousy because my life is horrible, I'm sure."

"I feel lousy because my family is mean."

"I feel lousy because *I'm* a loser."

Wrong, you feel lousy for a reason, and very likely that reason is unknown to you. Analyzing your life when feeling that way is emotional suicide, if you, like my client, get mad because you are mad because you are mad, etc. you will get worse. Simply say:

"I'm mad right now, but it will go away."

Moods happen for many reasons, accept them, don't dwell on them, judge them, argue with them, and they will go away.

4. Act as though you trust in your opinions.

Low self-esteem makes us insecure. Insecurity makes us uncertain when it comes to making decisions, because insecure people can be so fearful of making mistakes that they cannot make the simplest of decisions. They tell their subconscious minds the "*I am* wrong" message over and over, and if they think that their choices are not to be trusted, their self-worth becomes non-existent because they tie all their actions to other people's decisions and/or opinions.

The best way to overcome lack of confidence is through practice. Practice making decisions for yourself, but start small. Try rearranging your room or your living space a bit, and, even if you don't like it, leave it like that. Don't ask your roommate, partner, friend, children, parents, or pet for reinforcement. Don't ask, "Does the painting look good here? Or should I hang it 2 inches higher?" Decide for yourself and own the decision you have made. Practice shopping by yourself, and don't ask the sales person's opinion about the clothes you've tried on. If they don't make you smile, choose something else. If nothing makes you smile, choose the one that doesn't make you want to throw up. Sometimes I see very ugly clothes in the store … and I wonder who on this planet would buy them? If they thought nobody would buy them, they wouldn't sell it to start with. You are safe, no matter what, because whatever you choose to buy was chosen by somebody else who also thought that it was pretty.

A tough one here: Pretend not to be nervous when someone expresses disapproval. You may think that your self-consciousness is noticeable, but the truth is that practically no one is paying attention. Everyone is wrapped up in their own worries about their own perceived flaws, and I'm sure they haven't noticed anything about you. You do the same to others—you probably haven't noticed your coworkers' anxieties when you're focused on your own personal shame. If you keep pretending to believe in your own opinions for long enough (repetition), eventually you will completely believe in them.

Interesting fact: *Nicolaus Copernicus was a Polish astronomer and mathematician who got in trouble for discovering and claiming that the earth was not the center of the universe, but that the sun was. People who loved the previous theory were really mad about Copernicus' discovery. My hypothesis is that we earthlings love being the center of the universe, and that's why we think that everybody is noticing the way we dress, talk, or walk.*

We think that people notice the little stain on our blouse, our freckles, the way we blush, or any tiny little mistake we make as we go about our days. I suggest making a copy of this picture of Copernicus and put it in a place where you can see it. Maybe you also need a reminder that you are not the center of the universe and that people in your circles are more worried about getting your approval than in the little marinara stain on your white shirt.

Let me tell you a typical dialog that I have with most of the clients from the corporate world who come to see me:

"I need you to help me because I cannot speak up at company meetings."

"Why can't you?"

"Because I get too nervous."

"Why?"

"Because I am the most junior person on my team and I'm afraid of speaking up in front of my peers, who have more experience than me. If my ideas were good, somebody else would have come up with them, I'm afraid of saying something stupid."

"Suppose that you speak up and you say something stupid … so what?"

"So what? That would be terrible."

Bottom line: as a child he was punished for making mistakes and as an adult he cannot shake off those feelings of embarrassment.

Now, what happens when my client is not the most junior but one between levels?

"I need you to help me because I cannot speak up at company meetings."

"Why?"

"Because I get too nervous."

"Why?"

"Because people intimidate me, besides, the younger peers are full of fresh ideas, mixed with the experience of the more seasoned employees. It's like I'm trapped in a sandwich. What if I speak up and I say something stupid?"

"You say something stupid … so what?"

"So what? That would be terrible."

Bottom line: as a child he was punished for making mistakes and as an adult he cannot shake off those feelings of embarrassment.

Now this is what I get when my client happens to be the boss.

"I need you to help me because I cannot speak up at company meetings."

"Why?"

"Because I get too nervous."

"Why?"

"Because I am the boss and everybody looks up to me, imagine … the boss saying something stupid! That would be embarrassing! At least the lower levels can afford to look stupid right?"

"You say something stupid … so what?"

"So what? That would be terrible."

Bottom line: as a child he was punished for making mistakes and as an adult he cannot shake off those feelings of embarrassment. Sometimes, out of curiosity, I ask the 'boss' clients how, on this planet, they got to be a boss if they cannot speak up. This is what I always hear:

"Oh! Because my technical skills are awesome!"

I still fantasize, just like I did as a teenager with my Shaun-Cassidy-looking-Johnny-Lingo that I could get all the executives that come to see me together in a room, I would tell them that they all give me the same excuse of why they don't speak up in meetings. I'd make them hold hands and hug each other.

It's funny because sometimes when I see a client, who is wearing a badge and looks really smart and confident, I think:

"I don't think this charismatic guy is going to tell me that he is afraid in meetings." And there they are, doing exactly that: telling me that they get nervous in meetings … either because …

They blush

Or they have an accent like me

Or they think their teeth are ugly

Or they think their voice is squeaky

Or they run out of air

Or they are surrounded by geniuses

Or they think their hands are ugly

Or they have bunions

I'm amazed at the stories people tell me and, what's worse, they think those stories *are true*.

If this is your case, let me tell you. We are all in the same boat. We all have been scolded by some adult in our life, we all have been made fun of, we all have been rejected, neglected, put down, and we've all been disliked. It's like the ticket we need to get to be allowed on this planet. So, those people who intimidate you ... are also probably intimidated by you.

THOSE PEOPLE WHO INTIMIDATE YOU … ARE ALSO PROBABLY INTIMIDATED BY YOU

Still not convinced? Malcolm Gladwell, in his book *Outliers* describes the reason behind many plane crashes: "Being afraid of speaking up." The black boxes show the shaky voice of a shy copilot trying to hint that the airplane is going to crash or that the gas levels in the airplane are dangerously low.

They say it in such a polite and seeking approval tone that neither the captain nor the air traffic controllers take them seriously. Now they are dead, in addition to the innocent people who were in those airplanes.

"Mitigation explains one of the great anomalies of plane crashes. In commercial airlines, captains and first officers split the flying duties equally. But historically, crashes have been far more likely to happen when the captain is in the "flying seat." At first that seems to make no sense, since the captain is almost always the pilot with the most experience. But think about the Air Florida crash. If the first officer had been the captain, would he have hinted three times? No, he would have commanded—and the plane wouldn't have crashed. Planes are safer when the least experienced pilot is flying, because it means the second pilot isn't going to be afraid to speak up. Combating mitigation has become one of the great crusades in commercial aviation in the past fifteen years. Every major airline now has what is called "Crew Resource Management" training, which is designed to teach junior crew members how to communicate clearly and assertively. For example, many airlines teach a standardized procedure for copilots to challenge the pilot if he or she thinks something has gone terribly awry. ("Captain, I'm concerned about …" Then, "Captain, I'm uncomfortable with …" And if the captain still doesn't respond, "Captain, I believe the situation is unsafe." And if that fails, the first officer is required to take over the airplane.) Aviation experts will tell you that it is the success of this war on mitigation as much as anything else that accounts for the extraordinary decline in airline accidents in recent

years. "On a very simple level, one of the things we insist upon at my airline is that the first officer and the captain call each other by their first names," Ratwatte said. 'We think that helps. It's just harder to say, 'Captain, you're doing something wrong,' than to use a name."[14]

Pretend to trust your opinions, please. Your opinions are more reliable than you think. Believe me.

5. Use the nicest items you have

You don't have to go shopping, simply take out all those clothes in your closet that you've been saving for a special occasion. Today is the special occasion. You are the special occasion. Pull out those shoes and that sweater that you really love, wear your nice clothes every day. Get rid of the torn underwear, the socks with holes, and the clothing that you've never liked, because otherwise you are sending your subconscious mind the message of, *"It's only poor little me."*

It doesn't stop with clothing, either. Use the nice china. But, you may ask, what if I break it? Well, if you break it—you break it. If you die you will have to leave it behind, because I don't think it will fit in your coffin. Take out the nice silverware, and every item that you love that has been collecting dust for the last few years.

At first you will feel strange using that nice sweater or the china, but you have to constantly remind yourself that you are important and that you deserve good things. You need to create new neural pathways that will make positive changes in your life.

Wearing nice clothes doesn't mean that you have to pay a fortune for them. I have seen incredibly ugly clothes in designer stores and beautiful items in cheaper stores. The question is … will you feel happy wearing them? Will it make you feel good? Every time

[14] Outliers, Malcom Gladwell, Back Bay Books; Reprint edition (June 7, 2011)

you wear something nice, it's like you're saying, "*I am* very important, I only use nice things and I deserve it."

Look at your environment for events or coincidences that make you feel good about yourself. Hang on to any excuse that will make you feel good about yourself, and stop doing the opposite.

6. Stop over-apologizing

This one can be tricky, because, we have been trained to be polite and apologizing is part of the politeness menu. The problem is that we overdo it. We all want to be nice, and to be liked. Therefore, when in doubt: We apologize.

This is one of the most beautiful ads I've seen. Type on YouTube: "not sorry #shine strong Pantene."

It touched me because we, particularly women, tend to over-apologize, even for things that we haven't done. Somebody smashes our cart at the grocery store and we apologize. Why? Because we do it so much that it has become an automatic response. Sometimes it gets really annoying.

In a silent auction at my son's school I donated a soap-making class. Somebody bid on the class for her daughter and one day she came to take it. She was around 8 and she was charming. But she was trained to be polite to the point that she sounded fake and stiff. She said "thank you" more times than needed; every time she wanted to say something to me she said "excuse me," and every time she had a question about what to do next she apologized.

It sounded so unnatural, to the point that I was getting annoyed. I put up with it because I didn't want to spoil what her parents thought raising a polite little girl was, but if she had been my girl, I would have told her: "No more apologies here OK? You are perfect just the way you are. When you apologize too much your self-esteem goes down, and believe me my darling: We do not want that." Then she would have blushed and kept on apologizing until she got the hang of it, because nobody in my house is allowed to apologize unless there is a need for it.

It took us longer than expected to finish the soap, and I made her some lunch. Oh Gosh! Was she ever embarrassed! "Sorry! Sorry! Sorry!"

At some point I said:

"Sorry for what dear? I was the one who didn't plan how long it was going to take us to create the soaps, so, I am the one to blame for the delay, and I am not apologizing, but I want to feed you because you and I are hungry OK? It's a pleasure having you in my home. Just please enjoy and relax."

"Okay, thank you, and sorry" —she said while eating—of course I was already pulling my hair out of desperation.

When this girl's mom came to pick her up, we showed her the girl's creations. The mom was not impressed by the beautiful colorful soaps her daughter made and instead she asked her:

"Did you say 'thank you'?"

"Yes, mom."

"Did you say 'please'?"

"Yes, mom."

"Did you say 'I'm sorry' that she had to feed you? And I really apologize (she said to me) that you had to feed her, you shouldn't have."

I wanted to shake her by the shoulders and slap her, but I tried as hard as I could to keep a graceful composure. If I had been a normal person, I would just have said: "Oh, don't worry about it, Oh! You're very welcome! Oh! It was my pleasure!" But I couldn't do that because the hidden message she was telling her daughter was NOT OK. So, after she apologized for the millionth time that I had fed her girl I told her:

"So, what are you saying is that that because I didn't plan the soap-making timing well and she had to stay for lunch because she was hungry, you offended me?"

"Well no, but you didn't have to feed her."

What was she telling her daughter here? "You are not important, your needs are not important and whatever happens make sure people approve of you?"

When they left, the mom told the girl at least three times:

"So ... what do you say to Ms. Alba?" (I tell them to call me Ms. Alba because explaining how to pronounce my last name can be time consuming.)

"Thank you for the soaps!" the girl said again. (They paid for the soaps and the class.)

"And what else?"

"Thank you for feeding me!"

"And what else?"

"The food was delicious and you didn't have to feed me."

"And what else?"

"Good bye and nice meeting you! Ms. Alba!"

Then the mom proceeded to say those things to me over and

over. Like daughter like mother. She had trained her little one well. I didn't get to meet them, or know them. All I witnessed were those fake masks they put on to please me and make a good impression.

Over apologizing (repetition) gives our subconscious the following message:

> "I messed up, I messed up again, and again and again, please like me, I want to be acceptable in your eyes." Then the mind translates that into:

"*I am* not good enough, and I must be liked by the person who is in front of me no matter what."

Then those little girls and boys, grow up believing that they have to be liked, appreciated and even forgiven. That places their value as human beings in someone else's hands. Nobody is in charge of your value, or mine. You are the one in charge.

7. Carry yourself like a king (or queen)

I have had clients who tell me that entering a room full of people makes them very nervous. They feel like everybody is staring at them, which makes them self-conscious and terrified of tripping.

As you'll recall, when I was a teenager, I spent several months as an exchange student in Canada. When I came back to Mexico, my mother disapproved of my newfound demeanor and the new way I dressed; she was also mortified by how "rough and unfeminine" I had become. (I honestly don't remember being *that feminine* to start with.)

My father thought I was still the same sweet ol' me, but my mother took me to whichever training courses she deemed appropriate. I ended up in a class on how to become a lady again. The instructor was an elegant, nicely dressed and classy woman about my mother's age. They hit it off right away and that meant trouble for me; I'm sure she told my mom that she could do miracles with me. She showed us a lot of things, most of which I have long forgotten, but the ones that really stuck with me were the following two:

a) How to smoke with elegance.

As stupid as it may sound, I did pay attention to that. When I learned to smoke with my sister and cousins, I always made sure that I was doing it elegantly. My smoking charm lasted less than a year.

b) How to walk confidently.

The instructor first made us walk one by one while she and the rest of the class observed. We were so self-conscious and nervous that we looked awfully stiff. After we were done making a fool of ourselves, she explained, "The reason you were walking like limping storks is because you were nervous. You think you were nervous because the rest of us were staring at you, but that is not right. '*You were making yourself nervous by the things you were thinking.*' You were probably thinking something along the lines of, 'Oh God! This is embarrassing, am I doing it well? They are all staring at me and I am sure I am making a fool of myself.' Those thoughts projected themselves in your body language, which made you look insecure and uncoordinated."

Then she told us that we were going to walk in front of the group again, but that we were going to think the following:

"I am (your name here), my name is (your name here) and I am the very best."

So in my case it was, "I am Alba, my name is Alba and I am the very best."

"I am Alba, my name is Alba and I am the very best."

"I am Alba, my name is Alba and I am the very best."

I remember that the short little mantra made all the difference in the world. It was simple, memorable, and even fun. Because my mind was engaged *repeating* that, I didn't have much mental space left to be thinking about how awkward the whole thing was.

I was the first one because my last name starts with 'A'. As I was walking in front of the other classmates and thinking how I was the very best, I noticed that I was breathing more steadily, that my body was more relaxed, and that I was holding my chin a little higher.

I didn't need to stare at the floor. I was still a little nervous, but not nearly as much.

When I saw the other girls try it, I was bowled over! They looked like different people, walking graciously, with an elegant gait. They looked great, even a little cocky. The teacher asked us if we were nervous the second time, we all said "yes, but not as much." By looking at them I would have never guessed, not in a million years, that they were nervous. We were all happy and impressed at how well we did the second time around.

When my clients come and tell me that they need hypnosis because they feel very nervous when they enter a room full of people, (co-workers, upper management etc.), I tell them that they don't need hypnosis but a class on how to behave like a lady. I teach them the little mantra and after five minutes of practice they are ready. They love how it works. I also have offered to teach them how to smoke with elegance, but so far nobody has shown any interest.

8. Watch what you joke about

I like to joke around, sometimes a little too much. I like exaggerations, sarcasm and comical drama. Sometimes the jokes just pop into my head and I start laughing, right there, out of the blue.

I'm not the type of person who will simply say:

"I don't like how the soup I made turned out."

I would instead first scream … then when my kids and Jared, my husband, run to the kitchen to see if I'm still alive I'll tell them:

"This soup tastes like dirt. I'm going to throw up right now."

Then Fernando tastes it and says:

"Mom, what are you talking about? You just forgot to add salt."

"No, we have to check that there isn't a dead squirrel at the bottom."

He adds salt. Tries it, likes it, and says:

"Here mom. Much better." Then saying to his brother:

Fernando: "Mom is crazy."

Ivan: "I know. Jared, your wife is crazy."

Jared: "*I know*" Then he exchanges empathic looks with the dogs.

That's my story and family dynamics in a nutshell.

Now, it's important to mention that the subconscious mind doesn't have a sense of humor and it tends to take things literally. That has created me some problem with my jokes a couple of times.

First time

When the boys were little, we watched *Shrek 2* together. At some point in the movie, Shrek has an argument with the Fairy Godmother and points at her with his green fat finger. I remember saying right then to Fernando:

"Look! That's how you look when you are angry, and that's exactly how you point at me."

After that, every time Fernando was mad at me for something and he pointed at me as usual I'd tell him:

"Don't point at me with your green, fat Shrek finger!"

So, the green, fat, Shrek fingers became a family joke. It went on for months because every time that Fernando didn't like something he pointed at me.

One day Fernando woke up crying, and calling for me:

"MOM! I have a green, fat Shrek finger! ... and it hurts!"

There I went to check on him. And his index finger was swollen, it hurt and had a green hue to it.

"What happened?"

"I just bit out the loose skin around my fingernail."

"Wow! It's infected!" I said.

"It's your fault mom! For calling my fingers green, fat, Shrek fingers. Now it's stuck to my mind." (They have known the "stuck to my mind" sentence since they were lactating.)

I promised not to say "Shrek fingers" any more, but still, for a few months we had episodes of green infected fingers, some of them were so bad that it wouldn't go away with plain Neosporin. He had to see a doctor and take antibiotic. Then the finger infections stopped for good.

Was his mind trying to be nice to us and give him the fingers we jokingly requested with an **I am** statement? Probably.

Second time

Now that the boys are teenagers, they are a little too rough when they hug me. Jared is the same way. For some reason they think I enjoy playing lion cubs with them.

"I am not a guy, guys! I am a woman! And delicate, like a rose petal! (**I am** statement)". That's how the "rose petal" joke started. And mom was the rose petal. A delicate rose petal. Always delicate. Like a rose petal. They would hug me roughly and then they'd say: "Sorry mom, I didn't mean to hurt you, I forgot you are a rose petal, very delicate."

So, one day, the delicate rose petal—me—woke up with a rash on her skin. Belly, back, arms and legs. It was itchy as hell. I kept on wondering what kind of allergic reaction that was. The rash stayed for weeks. I tried removing different kinds of foods from my diet to get an idea of what was making my skin break out so much. Nothing. The rashes weren't going away, they were simply changing places. I checked my bed for spiders: nothing. I ended up in the allergist's office, so she would tell me what was going on. She gave me almost all the available tests to figure out my allergy. They all came out negative. No allergies.

"What do you mean *no allergies*?" I said.

"Your rashes aren't an allergic reaction to anything, I think they are eczema. Have you heard of eczema before?"

"No"

She started talking and explaining why some people get eczema and why others don't.

"Mainly, the people who get it are people who are born with a very *delicate skin.* You have to be very tender, don't scratch it when it's itchy, just pat it gently, don't use hot water in your shower, use lots of moisturizers, and pat it dry, never ever rub the towel on it."

I knew I didn't have delicate skin because I shower with boiling water, I don't use moisturizers and I love scratchy sponges. Also when I was pregnant, my belly itched so much that I enjoyed brushing it with a soft hair brush, that left my belly red and I knew I shouldn't have done it, but *Ah! it felt so good!* I don't even have one stretch mark on my belly. So, I know I have a strong skin.

Then I remembered my, "Delicate as a rose petal" jokes. I decided to stop the jokes. The skin problem went away. Was my mind trying to be nice to me and give me the skin I was asking for with my *I am* jokes? Probably. If you like joking, do not joke about life's little disappointments like:

The stupid drivers around you who didn't take driving lessons

Or when you are always in the slowest lane in the freeway

Or that everything that you eat makes you fat

Or that in the mornings your eyes look like a frog's

Or that a pain is sure sign that you are getting old

Stop any joke that has any negativity in it, no matter how funny it is.

Keep on joking, but use sarcasm instead:

I am always in the fastest lane in the freeway—today is just an exception.

Everything that I eat makes me look great

My morning eyes are my sexiest trait

Old? Me? At 90? You have to be kidding me. *I am,* look and feel incredibly young!

Interesting fact: *Talking about "old," don't let your age intimidate you, get used to the fact that many people will think you*

are old. When my boys were three days old, the doctor told me that I had to take them home. I asked why they couldn't stay any longer at the hospital's nursery. The doctor was very polite and he didn't want to use the "o" word. But I knew better.

9. Practice empathic singing

Before talking about singing, I want to make sure you realize the power of words and language. Consider placebo pills, for example. They work because a person is given an idea: "This medication will heal you." And based on his level of suggestibility, the pill will work.

If somebody tells you that you look pale, and asks you if you are all right, you will say, yes, I'm fine … and forget about it. Then, if a second person asks you if you are all right because you look pale, you'll say you are fine, but you'll start wondering a little. You go to a mirror and see that maybe you *are* a little pale.

You go on with your day. Then you come and see me and I tell you that you look very pale and ask you if you are feeling well.

"I do"—you will say—"but as a matter of fact, you are the third person who asked me that today." And as people keep on telling you that, you will start feeling sick, maybe dizzy or tired. You will go to the bathroom and see that you are really pale. Before you know it, you are in bed with some illness. Words have that power. The subconscious mind will take at face value any idea *repeated* over and over:

THE SUBCONSCIOUS MIND WILL TAKE AT FACE VALUE ANY IDEA REPEATED OVER AND OVER

Therefore let me inform you that the lyrics of the songs you sing in the shower or in the car are also ideas. Then, if it also happens to you, you will have the song that you were listening to in the car, stuck in your mind all morning.

I'm still passionate about the music from the '80s, and 90's and one of my favorite songs is "Creep" by Radiohead. The lyrics are absolutely depressing. I love the group, their style and the music of that song. Listen to it on YouTube (unless you have suicidal tendencies)

My point is that you shouldn't sing out loud music with angry or sad lyrics, because those lyrics are having an impact. But you like singing, just like me.

A solution is to look for songs in a foreign language or songs with happy lyrics, then you narrow down to two songs: La Macarena and Happy. The rest of the songs are along the lines of:

♫♪♫♪♫ I am nobody without you, so please don't leave me ♪♫♪♫

♪♫♪♫♪♫♪♫ If you leave me, I will die ♪♫♪♫♪♫♪♫

♪♫♪♫♪♫♪♫ Please come back to me or I'll die ♪♫♪♫♪♫♪♫

♪♫♪♫♪♫♪♫ Now that you left me, I will die ♪♫♪♫♪♫♪♫

♪♫♪♫You are thinking of leaving me, I'm thinking of dying ♪♫♪♫

And you like singing those! I do too. I don't want to listen to happy music all the time, but I don't want to confuse my mind by telling myself frequently that I love myself and then calling myself a creep when I'm singing in the car. The best way to deal with the problem is *to practice empathic singing.* Your favorite singer is sharing his music with you, those are his words and his feelings. Don't borrow his suffering. Acknowledge it, and sing it in a way that you leave the pain where it belongs: With the singer.

So if the song says:

"I am a nobody without you, so please don't leave me."

Change it to:

"You are a nobody without him ... so please don't leave her"

"If you leave me, I will die"

Change it to:

"If he leaves you, you will die."

"Without your love, I'm a nobody"

Change it to:

"Without his love, you are a nobody."

The heartbreak problem belongs to the singer. Don't grab it. Because the mind doesn't have sense of humor, if you sing a sad song in the first person, your mind will take notes. Because it wants to be good to you. Now you can sing whatever you want as long as you pay attention to change the "*I am*" parts of the song to "*You are.*"

Interesting fact: *I was raised Catholic, and for many years I wondered why we had to repeat (repetition) the prayers like a parrot. It felt meaningless and dumb. Jared is a Jew and I have been to the synagogue with him a few times. I see that Jewish congregations also*

repeat chants and prayers among other rituals. As I learn about the mind and about neural pathways I realize that even when our logical brain thinks that chanting is meaningless, our subconscious mind is taking those words at face value. I personally don't have the habit of praying or chanting, but I can see the logic behind the mantras and prayers that promote harmony and love: through repetition they hope to reach people and create empathic and peaceful communities.

"This book of the law shall not depart out of thy mouth, but thou shalt meditate thereon day and night, that thou mayest observe to do according to all that is written therein: for then thou shalt make thy way prosperous, and then thou shalt have good success."
Joshua 1:8

10. Say *thank you* when complimented

Is there anything more pathetic that somebody who doesn't take compliments gracefully? If I haven't seen it and heard it more often than I wished, I would have skipped this step. It's as simple as this: If somebody tells you what a nice sweater you are wearing,

Don't say: "This? I think it's horrible … I hate it … I got it in the Goodwill store … I only paid one dollar for it … I found it in a trash can."

Just say: "Thank you" (with a smile … if it's not too much to ask).

If somebody tells you what a nice house you have,

Don't say: "But it's a mess … but my husband doesn't let me paint it … but it's old … but it's falling apart … but we have termites."

Just say: "Thank you."

If somebody tells you that you look nice with your new haircut,

Don't say: "My hairdresser can make a frog look pretty … you are making fun of me … I hate it … I have split ends … I have a lot of grey hair … a bird just pooped on it."

Just say: "Thank you!"

If somebody tells you that your husband is nice.

Don't say: "You are kidding me right? He's a fat ugly slob ... he just got laid off ... he's getting old ..."

Just say: "Thank you."

If somebody tells you that your wife is nice,

Don't say: "You are kidding me right? She's a fat ugly slob ... she doesn't know how to cook ... she spends too much money on clothes."

Just say: "Thank you."

If somebody tells you that you play the piano really nicely,

Don't say: "This piano is out of tune ... I'm actually really bad ... My father always thought I was a lousy player."

Just say: "Thank you."

By saying "Thank you," you are taking the gift of the compliment gracefully; if you say anything under the "don't say" list, you will even make your friend uncomfortable and the conversation will have a sour tone to it.

You should work twice as hard when you are in love

When you are in love, the last thing you want to do is work on your self-esteem—you are already beaming, you look younger, your skin has a glow, you are naturally happy and the world becomes a better place, you bless the angry drivers around you and your sensitive buttons that people push to drive you crazy, suddenly disappear. People don't work on their self-esteem when they feel that way.

Been there, done that. One day, the day that the guy I had a crush on called me to ask me out, I just couldn't remove the smile from my face, not even in sad, neutral or even tragic situations. I could be watching the news about the starving children in China and I simply couldn't remove the smile. It was irremediably stuck.

I went to a gas station (in Mexico, you don't pump your own gas, you wait for somebody to help you and then you tip them), I was doing a business transaction, until the gas-pumping-guy couldn't help but ask:

"Can I ask why you are so happy? Is it your birthday today?"

I was going to start telling him my story, from beginning to end and how much I've waited for that darn call, but I saw that there were cars behind me waiting to be filled too.

I just simply said:

"Yes, today is my birthday."

"Well, happy birthday then."

That day I smiled so much that my cheeks were hurting. (Has that happened to you? I hope so). When you are in love, the last thing you need is something to make you feel good about yourself; you already feel awesome. Still, you do need to work on your self-esteem when you are in love for many reasons:

To prevent yourself from doing something stupid, like flying to Las Vegas and having an Elvis Presley marry you, when you don't even know the guy's (or girl's) last name.

To avoid getting pregnant when you don't want to.

To avoid having your parents, friends or even me tell you: "I told you so."

To avoid the roller coaster moods: He calls, you are in heaven; he doesn't call, you are in hell; he calls, you are back in heaven; he arrives late, you are back in hell.

To set healthy limits and not get taken for granted.

My experience with guys is that they don't lose it as much as we women do, but I have seen exceptions. I know that you are not going to listen to me, because when I'm in love I don't work on my self-esteem either. Even when I don't follow my own advice, it's my moral obligation to warn you. If you don't work on your self-esteem when you are in love, your self-worth changes owners. It stops belonging to you and it starts belonging to your boyfriend or lover.

By the time I was in my 20s, I had a clear idea of how to keep my self-esteem high, and I was constantly working on making a conscious effort to have positive and uplifting thoughts. And then, I fell in love and immediately forgot to keep working on myself. It was in a class I was taking in College, his name was Guillo (short for Guillermo) and he took the classes with me.

He liked studying with me because I was a good student and he wasn't. I loved studying with him because just having him there, sitting next to me, would make my heart sing and my mouth drool. Thoughts about him filled most of my waking time. He wanted to study with me very frequently, and I'd always say "Yes." Sometimes he wanted to study longer hours than I was comfortable with, but he never seemed to know the material, and I did love helping him.

There were many days where we studied together until around 1:00 or 2:00 AM. I shared my notes with him, and I was there when he needed me. I was wrapped up in making Guillo happy. In the class was a beautiful girl named Remy. She got very good grades too, and I knew that sometimes Guillo asked her if they could study together. "No," she'd say. "I already studied, and I have other plans for tonight." Then Guillo would ask me. And I would say "Yes."

"Give him what he wants and he'll prefer me over Remy," I thought.

Then he started asking me for quick dates, like at a coffee shop. We had wonderful conversations and I was in the clouds. Then he started asking me to lend him some money here and there. We'd meet for lunch at the cafeteria and then he'd ask me to buy him lunch.

Sometimes I thought he was asking for more than he was giving, because I was always the one doing favors for him. I let him borrow my notes, studied with him, and lent him money which I never got back. If he called me at the last minute to get together or to study together, I'd drop *everything*. I was always Alba to the rescue for him, for months.

I kept on thinking, "Why won't he love me? I give him whatever he wants." Until one day, I was eavesdropping in class and heard Remy say to her girlfriends, "I finally said 'Yes' to Guillo. He's been insisting a lot."

When I found out that Guillo and Remy were dating, I was very, *very* sad. If you've had your heart broken you know what I'm talking about. They were always together and I was feeling sick. He forgot about me, and to make matters worse I was always running into them when they were gazing into each other's eyes with total adoration. I was convinced that I was broken because Guillo didn't choose me. He didn't want to study with me anymore, and in the cafeteria, he was always with her. I felt used. How dare he? After all I'd done for him! She didn't let him study with her if it was not convenient for her. She never lent him money. And yet, he was with her and not me!

As a result, my self-esteem dropped; my balloon was deflated and flat. I was so sad that I was having a terrible time keeping up with my studies, because I just couldn't focus. I had been crying so much that my cheeks were getting vertical red lines that started in the corner of my eyes and ended on my jaw, and those lines hurt, so I had to cover them with Vaseline if I wanted to keep on crying. At some point I wasn't sure if I was crying because of my heartbreak or my *cheek break*. I was even angry at myself for crying so much.

"Okay woman! Put yourself together! You have to do something about it," I thought. And then I remembered ... "Ah! My self-esteem! I forgot!" I knew I had to work on my self-esteem, because my misery was unbearable. If your heart has been broken you know what it feels like, and it is not fun. So I wrote myself a love letter, and I read it to myself every night. Mine in a nutshell was something like this:

"*I, Alba, **am** gorgeous, smart, valuable, fun, adorable, sexy. I **am** important, I love myself so much, I look in the mirror and I smile. I **am** healthy, creative, charismatic, witty and fun. **I am** a lovely princess.*" In addition to reading my love letter, I was also constantly paying attention to my inner dialog. Every time I caught myself saying, "How stupid you are," or dwelling on the "poor me, nobody loves me" pattern, I had to make a conscious effort to say: "Alba shut up, **you are** smart, beautiful, valuable, sexy, creative, charismatic and funny."

I was surprised to realize how often I was telling myself awful stuff. How on earth was I going to feel good about myself if my little voice was constantly shooting angry bullets into my heart? The fact that Guillo left me for Remy had no meaning—it was my inner dialog that was driving me crazy. Anyway, the first time I read my love letter, I didn't believe a word I wrote. I didn't believe I was valuable, gorgeous, fun, sexy, intelligent, and adorable. I was not a princess—I was hideous, dumb, and a stupid doormat. That's how I really felt.

But the point here is not to believe those nice words, the point is to read them. Period. I "knew" that those nice words were lies. But I also knew that those *lies* would eventually sink in.

At first, reading my love letter was hard, because I didn't believe any of that, so it made me feel like a narcissistic liar. And also because it was hard to allocate one part of my brain to pay constant attention to my self-talk, especially at the beginning, when the self-harassment and sadness were frequent. After a week, it was easier to read the love letter. Instead of feeling like an impostor, it was more like, "*whatever.*" And it was not as hard to pinpoint negativity and to switch to positive words.

After two weeks, it was even easier to read the letter. For some reason those words didn't feel alien any more. Why would they? I'd been reading them for a while and my belief system was beginning to change because of the repetition. And after three weeks (yes, three weeks), I was beaming, I was mainly in a good mood, and I felt great about myself. I was back at my studies, working hard on my classes, and being friendly towards my classmates.

In the midst of my joy, I was skipping around in the cafeteria when I stumbled into Guillo, who had come to talk to me. I was surprised but pleased to realize that I was neither shaking nor drooling. I kept my poise as I stood waiting for him to talk.

"Hey, Alba, could you lend me money, please? I'm short on cash right now."

"No, I don't want to lend you money because you never pay me back."

"Do you want to study together tonight?"

"No, I've already studied, so I have other plans."

I found out later that Remy had broken up with him. And I don't take anyone's leftovers. After he left, all I could think was, "Oh yeah, baby! I was brave, big time brave! Good for me!" And I went skipping to class. He went away and never came back. He was crazy for Remy, and they kept on going out and breaking up for the rest of the term. They didn't get married, but he ended up marrying somebody who looked like Remy's twin.

Another reason to work on your self-esteem when you are in love is because it will help you feel confident and happy, and that will make your partner happy because everybody loves dating somebody happy and confident. No one likes doormats, and that's exactly what happened to me with Guillo. I was his *okeydokey* girl. No wonder he didn't take me seriously. Feeling great about yourself will also help you pinpoint right away when your loved one is being a little disrespectful or rude, so you speak up. Not speaking up makes us lose respect for ourselves, and our loved ones lose respect for us too. Nobody will see anything in you that you don't already have.

There aren't Johnny Lingos out there. If you don't think you are great-looking, smart, sexy, charming, adorable, and assertive, nobody else will either. What's even better is how people will start treating you differently, once you've gotten into the habit of loving yourself. As you treat yourself better, others will treat you better. If you convince yourself by repetition, do nice things for yourself, and treat yourself as somebody important, you will eventually start believing that you are a wonderful nine-cow woman or man. What if, instead of clinging to excuses to feel broken, we clung to excuses to feel complete and worthy?

You need to do that for yourself. If you wait for somebody to rescue you, or if you wait for somebody to make you feel great about yourself, your self-esteem will be built on a very weak foundation, because it'll have been built by another person's hands. You can end up, little by little, feeling broken if things don't work out. This happened to me with Guillo, with Edgar, and to Leslie Morgan with her ex-husband.

How can this information be useful?

Remember that there are no innocent words, and that the mind assimilates everything you say repeatedly because it understands the language, but it doesn't have a sense of humor. Remember to work on your self-esteem when you are in love. Remember to practice the self-esteem work out. You will be amazed with the results.

WHICH ONE ARE YOU?

Chapter 10

Life in a Tribe

"I am free, no matter what rules surround me. If I find them tolerable, I tolerate them; if I find them too obnoxious, I break them. I am free because I know that I alone am morally responsible for everything I do."
Robert A. Heinlein

Now let's discuss our interactions with others and why they have a major influence on our self-esteem. Specifically, I will be covering the importance of being assertive and having a backbone. For every little abuse we endure, our self-esteem goes down a little.

It's true that there are people who can let negative comments and criticism slide away. But there are far, far more people who wish that their tormentor would move to the other side of the world, because they're greatly affected by this person's persistent little aggressions, constant requests, and back-handed insults. The moment people feel empowered and speak up is the moment that their self-esteem starts soaring. It's when they fully realize that they are important and that their needs, space, time and preferences are important too.

Humans are pack animals. The species has evolved to want to make other members of their tribe happy. In prehistoric times, people needed to be part of a group that provided them shelter, protection and food. They also had responsibilities within their group; broadly speaking, females were responsible for gathering fruit, and males were responsible for hunting. If there was a bully, inside or outside the group, the alpha male would protect the tribe, the group was in charge of maintaining a safe environment, and individuals needed to comply with the will of the group. If the alpha male was the bully, the group members had to put up with it if they didn't want to be kicked out of the tribe. They instinctively knew that, without the protection of the group, their chances of survival were terrifyingly low. Back then, losing the tribe meant not only isolation, but almost certain death by a hungry predator or starvation. At a primitive level, the fear of exclusion and rejection is tied to isolation and danger.

Now, let's fast forward to the modern age. Isolated groups in the wild are no longer the norm but have become the exception. We are in a world where babies keep popping out faster than popcorn, where an average of 250 babies are born every minute and where a significant majority of those infants will survive to maturity. Some nations are overcrowded because people have followed their survival instincts incredibly well. Now we live in communities, but rejection from those communities won't guarantee death, or even a poor life. Yet we still feel a lot of pain when we're rejected, because our primitive brain still thinks we live in prehistoric times.

Isolation or rejection can mean death. That's what our emotional brain feels, even if our logical brain knows that this isn't the case anymore. The logical brain tries to reason with the emotional brain, the two of them don't communicate well. This happens because when our survival is endangered—either in a perceived or real manner—our subconscious mind is designed to take over and leave logic behind.

If we want to have a good self-esteem and follow our dreams, our tribe isn't wired to help. Our tribe—all tribes—have the group wiring of "The chain is as strong as its weakest link." Tribes need uniformity and compliance to survive; there has to be order. In ancient times, tribes had different methods of distinguishing one tribe from another.

A modern example is sports teams. You might not be able to see their faces from afar, but you can sure see the color of their uniforms that indicate "my team" or "the opponent's team." If you want to drive two teams crazy (and the spectators too), make them wear the exact same uniform.

And this doesn't only apply to groupings like teams. Back in prehistoric times, if a person looked too different from afar, the hunters in a tribe could have hunted them down, thinking that they could pose a threat. So if there were rules to follow, you had to follow them. If there were fashion trends in your tribe, you had to follow them too.

I like to imagine teenage girls back then trying to look as different as possible from their tribe and driving the adults crazy. "If you don't look like us, how will we be able to tell you apart from the enemy?" I can picture a prehistoric mom scolding her teenage daughter when she wants to try a different clothing style:

"We all wear tiger clothes and its final. I don't care how cute the zebra dress you made is!" And the teenage daughter would throw a fit because she wants to wear a zebra dress instead. If the teenagers back then were anything like many of the teenagers nowadays, I could see a situation like that happening.

But in those times, conformity was a survival mechanism. If all of the members of the tribe got to choose their own colors, they would go crazy trying to distinguish friend from foe. Therefore wearing that zebra skin was out of the question.

That's why we have to fight stereotypes. Your logical brain is trained and knows that all people are valuable regardless of their race, religion, cultural background, age, shape and color. But if you happen to be alone at night and a group of people who look similar to each other but different than you approach you, that primitive survival mechanism within you will kick in. If that group has people who are much taller and look stronger and faster ... I can see you hyperventilating already. Now, even though times have changed, tribes still push us to conform.

Culture shock

I was raised in Mexico City in a community that pays a lot of attention to appearances. You have to dress nicely, similar to some big cities in Europe. You have to wear nice, clean and trendy clothes. I thought that that was the norm everywhere, not just in Mexico City. But when I moved to Saskatchewan in Canada for a year, I realized that I was wrong. I packed my city clothes, and off I went to a rural area. When I landed in Regina, I was surprised to see that *everybody was a cowboy*!

"Wow, *they* are so different," I thought. I actually felt like I was inside a cowboy movie. Here I was, with my suit and my high heels without realizing that I was the one who was different and out of place, not them.

As the months went by, my uniform changed and I transformed from a city girl to a cowgirl. And I loved it. I loved the simple openness of the people, and I loved the sense of community. It was like a big family (gossip included) and, slowly but surely, I blended in. I became one of them and my city clothes made me feel like a ridiculous snob. I even wore an anklet that a friend gave me.

After I stepped out of my own tribe in Mexico City, I could realize how snooty the neighborhood I was raised in really was. It was so obvious from the outside, even though it seemed so normal from the inside. When I came back to Mexico, I was a real cowgirl, and I was going to stay that way. I wanted to stay simple and to love people for who they were, not for what they looked like or how classy they dressed. My new anti-uniform was jeans and plaid shirts. Until my mom saw the clothes that I had in the suitcase and the anklet I was wearing and put her foot down. "You will not find a decent husband wearing that," she told me. "There aren't any cowboys for you here, so kiss your farm clothes and your anklet goodbye."

My whole suitcase full of clothes ended up being donated to charity. She took me shopping; she registered me into the "How to be a lady again" classes, and there I was, against my will, a city girl again. "But Mom! I love my anklet and my cowboy boots and my cowboy hat! Dressing like that makes me happy." That was my complaint, but it didn't make any difference whatsoever. Again, the tribe doesn't care if your self-esteem is high or if you are happy. The tribe is wired to protect its integrity.

Tribes have survived through the years by following certain patterns, by wearing similar clothes, by having certain religions and believing in certain political ideas. Tribes are not designed to be open-minded, supportive and cool.

Why change things that are working for us right now? That sentiment is part of why it took so much work to abolish slavery. It's part of why it took a lot of work to allow women to vote, etc. Societies don't like change, and they will sometimes do terrible things to maintain the status quo.

THEN   ...AND NOW

In this family, we all get PhDs.

In this community, we all play sports.

In this community, we have all the babies that God *sends* us.

In this family, we are all dancers.

In this society, we worship this or that God.

In this society, being single … fat … gay … divorced … is completely unacceptable.

In this society, women are objects.

In this society, we tell you who you will marry.

In this community, men don't wash dishes or change diapers.

In this community, women don't go out alone without their husbands' permission.

And we expect you to comply.

It's sad to realize that, in some tribes, certain horrific rituals and criminal acts are still considered normal.

Beyond this, there are other subtle but also irrational beliefs that can be passed from one generation to another.

All the women in our family with green eyes have bad luck with guys.

All the men of our family die before turning fifty.

Nobody in this family is or has ever been smart.

In this family, we take over the family business, we don't choose our careers.

In this family, we die of skin … pancreatic … liver … cancer.

In this family, somebody always drowns.

In this family, we are all athletes (god forbid that you are an intellectual).

In this family, we are all intellectuals (god forbid that you are an athlete).

Beliefs like these can dictate the course of people's lives and their relationships with the people around them.

Have you ever watched the movie *October Sky*? (Spoiler alert.) The film takes place in Coal wood, West Virginia in October 1957, and is based on the true story of Homer Hickam. Coal mining was the town's livelihood, and almost every man in the town worked in the mines. But Homer, the main character, had other plans. The launch of the Russian satellite Sputnik in October 1957 was a turning point in his life. The movie is about his obsession with building a rocket and becoming a scientist, and the rejection he encounters from his father, the school principal, some of his friends and many men in the town, who believed that "If we've been miners all of our lives and we've done just fine, what's wrong with that? And ... why change it?"

So, if a chain is only as strong as its weakest link, and that link is a boy who is not willing to conform, why should the town be supportive? If they are supportive, there will likely be more kids like him wanting to do something different with their lives. By that logic, eventually there won't be any more miners, and the livelihood of the town will disappear.

It's not that they are evil people who don't want Homer to fulfill his dreams; they are collectively fighting to maintain the integrity and homeostasis of the tribe. So, at this point, everybody cares less about Homer's happiness and self-esteem than about his compliance. They know mining, and a future without mining is frightening to them. That's why, in the movie, Homer is repeatedly asked, "What's wrong with being a miner?"

In my mother's mind, if I wore a certain style of clothes, she would know what kind of suitors I would get. God knows who I might end up with wearing cowboy clothes in a city that hasn't ever seen a cow.

The bottom line is: Your tribe is not wired to make an isolated member happy. Your tribe (and any tribe) wants to preserve its integrity and stability by having everyone in it comply. That's why you get lessons like "You are not good enough if your performance is not appropriate."

Therefore, on one side of the coin, we get the psychologists' ideas of, "You are complete for who you are, you are perfect for who you are, you are lovable and worthy for who you are." (Those ideas come from the logical brain)

But in the meantime, you will feel absolutely miserable if you make mistakes, because your society will pay more attention to your failures than to your successes. That's when you learn—because you learn very well—to be hard on yourself when you make a mistake (automatic reaction from your subconscious mind).

And we wonder how people start verbally or mentally abusing themselves. We want to receive approval from our peers, and in order to be approved of, we need to perform well and do almost everything right. Liking ourselves is not a quality that will earn us any extra points with the tribe.

The approval of the tribe comes from our compliance with its rules, traditions and expectations. So, if you want to have high self-esteem and goals, you will have to work for it, since the tribe won't provide it for you. You will have to work harder not only to earn the tribe's respect, but also to avoid the tribe's disdain, because the negativity bias will make your tribe focus on what's wrong with you or your behavior and probably judge you as a result. The negativity bias will make your tribe members pay more attention to the negative, and their generalizations will lead them (and you) to draw mean and inaccurate conclusions.

Negativity Bias:

You say: I have a goal.

Your tribe hears: I am rebellious and I don't want to do as I'm told.

Generalization:

You say: I have a goal.

The tribe hears: I am a troublemaker and a rebel.

There's another reason that makes the tribe reject the idea and that's called "ego." You say: "I have a goal." They hear: "You are a bunch of losers and the last thing I want is to be like you." Then they feel offended and attack you in subtle or not-so-subtle ways, because they think that you attacked them first by calling them losers. You never called them losers and you wonder what all the fuss is about. My own opinion of all of this? I think that human interactions are wonderful, incredibly complex and borderline grotesque at the same time.

If there's a tradition that's specific to a tribe, the group will push to keep that tradition alive for the sake of the tribal identity and integrity. That's why some groups, especially when they move to a different country, do things like rejecting the American boyfriend of the Japanese daughter. Why? Because it's a threat to the overall identity of the group, which is wired to stay together and maintain homeostasis.

That's why if we make a mistake, the group may respond by expressing disapproval, and as children, many of us were criticized, yelled at and scolded by our groups. Of course, if we are scolded we often feel bad, and if we feel bad our self-esteem falls. That's how we started associating our self-esteem with what we do, not with who we are. As sad as it is, it happens to all of us over and over again, until eventually our self-worth depends on our tribe's approval because we're driven by the subconscious fear of being kicked out.

*   *   *

The Stanford prison experiment

In 1971, psychologist Philip Zimbardo conducted what ended up being a highly controversial experiment. His research involved analyzing the participants' behavior in a simulated prison environment. Their goal was to see if good people would change their behavior and values if the environment allowed it.

Zimbardo and his researchers created a simulated prison in the basement of the Stanford University psychology building. Then they chose 24 undergraduate students to be either pretend guards or pretend prisoners. They chose those 24 students carefully to make sure they were physically and emotionally healthy, with no emotional or psychological issues. Zimbardo knew they had good apples and they were going to put them in a bad position that's a prescription for abuse: power without oversight.

The mock prison had cells, and the prisoners were randomly assigned cells that they had to stay in day and night. Guards worked in shifts, and were allowed to go to their dorms or back home until their next shift. The behavior of both sets of participants was recorded with hidden cameras.

The experiment was supposed to last two weeks, but it had to be stopped prematurely because the situation took an unexpected turn. The majority of the guards started to behave in ways that were abusive towards the inmates, while the inmates became passive and had emotional breakdowns within 36 hours.

They experienced crying episodes and high levels of stress. Zimbardo demonstrated how people can change their behavior, depending on the setting that they are placed in. The guards, who were placed in a position of power, behaved in ways alien to their previously observed personalities. Meanwhile, the prisoners shut down and ceased functioning, even though they knew they could leave the experiment whenever they felt uncomfortable. Still, during the experiment they forgot their rights and decided to shut down instead of just leave.

This experiment puzzled the researchers: Why, if the prisoners knew that they had a choice to leave, did they stay? What made them forget their rights? At a primitive level, we are wired to shut down when confronted or held hostage, to cooperate with our captors to survive. But these Stanford students knew that they could leave if they chose to, yet they didn't do so despite repeated reminders and their own obvious suffering. All I can think of is that, for the mind, perception is reality, and for them, at some point they began to obey the emotional, primitive part of their brain that told them to "Stay put and comply," instead of the logical part that said, "Get out of this experiment and go back to your dorm."

"So what are the seven social processes that grease the slippery slope of evil? Mindlessly taking the first small step. Dehumanization of others. De-individuation of self. Diffusion of personal responsibility. Blind obedience to authority. Uncritical

conformity to group norms. Passive tolerance of evil through inaction or indifference.

And it happens when you're in a new or unfamiliar situation. Your habitual response patterns don't work. Your personality and morality are disengaged. So situations have the power to inflame the hostile imagination in some of us, that makes us perpetrators of evil, can inspire the heroic imagination in others. It's the same situation. And you're on one side or the other. Most people are guilty of the evil of inaction, because your mother said, "Don't get involved. Mind your own business." And you have to say, "Mama, humanity is my business." [15]

The experiment also shows that we are more likely to get away with stuff if we are put in a position that allows us to.

This experiment is an extreme case, but occasionally I notice a variation of the theme on a smaller scale. Some of my clients let others get away with abuse. They feel trapped as though they truly had no choice, like an employee who thinks he has to put up with a verbally abusive boss. Sometimes they are so used to it that they don't even notice.

One night I was having dinner at a friend's house and my friend asked her daughter if she wanted to eat. Her daughter's response was this: "No! And shut up, mom!"

"OK. Maybe later," my friend said.

Before I knew it I found myself saying, "Why do you let your kid talk to you *that* way?" The moment I said it I regretted it, but what surprised me most was my friend's response.

"What way?"

[15] Zimbardo, P. (2008, February). Philip Zimbardo: The psychology of evil [video file]. Retrieved from http://www.ted.com/talks/philip_zimbardo_on_the_psychology_of_evil

As I felt the blood rush to my face, I ended up saying, "Nothing, never mind," and then glaring at the little brat. In the meantime, my friend looked at me with a clueless face and repeated, "What are you talking about, you know kids nowadays."

We shut down when we have to deal with an uncomfortable situation and would rather not speak up. It's the status quo and it's hard to change. What I have seen with my clients is that when I ask them why they don't speak up, the common answer is: "I feel guilty if I do because I don't want to hurt the abuser's feelings."

We feel guilty for not being nice enough, we feel guilty for saying "no" and, in some cases, we feel terrified to speak up even when the abuse is more than obvious. We are afraid of ridicule and try to keep our composure and not show our vulnerabilities or weaknesses. We also prefer to put up with abuse because we don't want to be perceived as weak. "Oh, his behavior doesn't bother me at all" somebody says, faking a smile. "I am strong, he is the weird one, I just play along." You just play along? No, you don't, you are afraid of speaking up.

Why? Because we don't want to be rejected by the tribe, whether that tribe is real or imagined. Many of us would rather be abused than be rejected.

I'll cover many variations of the same topic, hoping that you'll find one that is right for you. There is nothing wrong with wanting to make everybody happy, as long as the driving force behind your actions is love and not fear.

THERE IS NOTHING WRONG WITH WANTING TO MAKE EVERYBODY HAPPY AS LONG AS THE DRIVING FORCE BEHIND YOUR ACTIONS IS LOVE AND NOT FEAR

But ... When should you speak up?

If making others happy interferes with your goals, you have to do something about it.

If making others happy means that you say "yes" when you wished you said "no" … you have to do something about it.

If somebody wants something from you that you don't want to give, you have to do something about it.

If somebody's level of intimacy is making you uncomfortable, you have to do something about it.

If making others happy means that you have to put up with abuse, whether physical or emotional, you have to do something about it!

But … and this is very important: If you want to make a sacrifice for that person's sake … go for it! If you are doing it for love … do it. If you are doing it for fear … don't do it. If in your heart it feels good to do it … do it … if it doesn't … don't do it. Sometimes we have to do sacrifices for our loved ones, such as taking care of an elderly parent, sibling or friend. But you know in your heart that you are doing it with love, not with resentment. If it doesn't feel good in your heart, you have to do something about it. Why?

Because you owe it to yourself.

Because you despise yourself for not doing anything.

Because the resentment is unhealthy for your body.

Because when you do speak up, the relationship doesn't disappear, it just balances out.

A lot of people tell me "I prefer to put up with my relative's abuse because I don't want to alienate them." Speaking up won't alienate them, it will make them stay, but will also make them realize that your boundaries have to be respected. If, by chance, you lose that person the moment you speak up, let me tell you: You don't need that person in your life, the same way you don't need cigarettes or drugs. And the most important reason why you have to do something about it is: Because the other party making demands doesn't think you are nice.

I am still waiting to meet a manipulator who thinks highly of the manipulated one. They would say things like "He's such a wimp."

Or "He's got no backbone." Or "I kind of like him because I can get away with stuff, and he's a pushover."

One day I was with a friend at her parent's house. Her 35-year-old adult brother lived there at the time. Their mom was serving us dinner, and suddenly, out of the blue, he started yelling aggressively at his mom because he found a hair in his soup. He tossed the spoon on the floor and kept on yelling." She apologized and went to the kitchen to replace his bowl of soup.

I was so startled by that, I reacted the same way I did as a child when my parents or a teacher yelled at me: I started sobbing.

When he saw me, he said, "You made Alba cry, Mom. She is disgusted by that hair in the soup too." (His objective assessment of the situation.)

I finally told him "Why are you so mean to your mom? That was very rude." And you know what he said? He didn't say, "Oh, she's such a wonderful person and I really admire her." No, he said, "She loves being a slave." (**I am** statement)

As much as I disliked him, I must confess that he was right about that. The one who was wrong was the mom, who thought that she was being such a loving mom.

Now, the other side of the coin. When a manipulator finds somebody strong who won't put up with any kind of abuse, not even a little bit, they form opinions like:

"He is very important."

"She doesn't take shit from anyone."

"He has my respect."

"She says 'No' a lot, but I understand, because she's very busy."

"He has great self-esteem."

So if you think that you are being loved, popular and virtuous for saying "yes" to every request, I've got bad news for you. It is more likely that you will be loved and respected if you come across as strong, if you assert your rights and if you don't give in to other people's demands.

At some point in my early teens I was extremely shy, and believing that my nose made me hideous didn't help. That made me the perfect candidate for being picked on at school. I was terrified of my bullies, but I never said or did anything. In addition to that, I was going to religious classes several evenings a week, and those classes were from a branch of the church that turned out to be very manipulative.

They used biblical quotes to control us, like the one of Jesus and the cheek, that we should fear God's wrath, and that I was going directly to hell if I didn't do this and that. I was being trained by them to be submissive and obey their orders, and I did for a while. So I had this completely malformed idea that I was a doormat because Jesus said so and because I didn't want God's wrath in my life. I wanted to feel virtuous because I thought I was being a good Catholic girl, but something felt very wrong inside. I was constantly afraid and my stress levels were very high.

One day I said that's it, cut myself off from religion and decided to study more about the mind. I tossed my bible in the depths of my closet and started looking for other ideas. That's when the book Your Erroneous Zones by Wayne Dyer came in handy:

"Self-esteem? What? It's not a sin? WOW!"

So I decided to break free from religion. The funny thing is that even when I proclaimed myself to be an atheist, I still prayed at night. "Dear Jesus, I don't want to go to church any more because now I'm an atheist, the truth is that I'm mad at you and at your stupid cheek because it causes me a lot of problems, but please don't tell God because I don't want to burn in hell. Please look after my mom, my dad, my brother, my sister and me. In the name of the Father, the Son and the Holy Spirit, amen."

As years went by, the mystery of the cheek kept me wondering because it didn't make sense. I thought highly of Jesus but that quote just took away many popularity points from him.

Until not too long ago … it clicked … it was more like a bat hitting me on the head than an innocent click, because it came as an epiphany. *The cheek quote is about being brave, not about being a coward!* You probably have known this for years, but for me it was a total revelation. The other cheek is not an invitation to be abused, it's not a "Please hit me, I'm a nobody, you can do with me whatever you want." The Bible doesn't say: "Give the other cheek and then lay down on the floor so they can step all over you." It's more along the lines of: "I am strong, I have a deep conviction and you can slap me all you want because I'm not afraid of you and you won't stop me." The other cheek is about being brave with dignity and conviction like Malala, Rosa Parks and Martin Luther King. (In case you were wondering, Jesus got his popularity points back.)

*   *   *

One of my favorite books and a huge eye opener

Sherry Argov, the author of *Why Men Love Bitches* and *Why Men Marry Bitches*, doesn't get tired of reminding us that being overly nice will make the guy of our dreams walk away. Any decent man who is looking to settle down will not settle for someone who's willing to say "Yes" to all of his requests. He may like that she says "Yes" to everything, but he won't take her seriously. According to Argov's books, a guy worth his salt will choose a confident woman who doesn't take crap from anyone (not even from him) and is not afraid to voice her needs or say "No."

Her books gave me the answer (way too late, I must admit) of why, when I was a teenager and I had a crush on someone, the guy wanted nothing to do with me, and why the ones who had crushes on me were the ones I wanted nothing to do with. I was a doormat for the guys I was interested in, and that kept me from catching their interest. And still I wondered: "Why doesn't he like me? After all the nice things that I do for him, the brownies I bake for him? Nobody is nicer to him than me. What's wrong with *him*?"

Back then, I didn't know that the one who was totally wrong in her behavior was yours truly. Had I known this back then, I wouldn't have suffered nearly as much heartbreak as I did. As Argov puts it:

> "A smart, together guy won't build a life with a woman he feels doesn't have her feet firmly planted on the ground. Men do not marry the 'little girl' types because they don't want to feel like they are adopting a young child. The only reason men like stupid women is so they can take advantage of them—in the short term. A quality guy worth his salt wants a partner who is competent and multidimensional. Someone who can handle things when he's not around."[16]

The conclusion of her books is this: if you want men to like you, you don't have to work hard at being liked, you have to work hard at liking yourself. When you like yourself, you set boundaries, you say "No," and you display self-esteem and self-respect. And in the end, the guys who are worth it will like you more. The same applies to men who are seeking female partners in their lives. I have seen male clients who struggle to get a partner and who don't understand why women don't find them appealing, despite their "caring, sweet, giving and loving nature." They fail to understand that they're being too accommodating and that women respect men who are willing to stand up for themselves.

In the end, it's important to accept reality, and you may have to do the hard thing and confront the important people in your life, even though they may not like it. The point is that despite all of the obstacles in your path, the end result is worth it.

How can this information be useful?

When you want to achieve something, you may face rejection from your group, but don't take it personally, that's their role. But now you

---

[16] Argov, S. (2006). *Why Men Marry Bitches: A Woman's Guide to Winning Her Man's Heart.* New York: Simon & Schuster Paperbacks.

know better. Besides, if you show them how serious you are, they will adapt. Change is a hard concept for them to assimilate.

Realize that sometimes people will try to get away with things if you let them. One of the key ingredients of a good self-esteem is the ability to set healthy boundaries and not put up with any kind of abuse. Remember that offering a helping hand doesn't make you a wimp, because your drive is love and not fear. Fear not only lowers our self-esteem and makes us more prone to be abused by others, but in extremes, fear of speaking up makes us weak and unable to take action when a strong stance is needed. Remember the previous example of why some plane crashes happen, simply because the copilots were afraid to speak up. If we don't exercise the backbone muscle, and if a serious situation strikes, we won't be able to handle it, because we will be overwhelmed by insecurities. In a serious situation, we can be one of two things: a coward or a hero—we cannot be both. Exercise your bravery muscle so you are prepared to become a hero when the situation requires it.

Chapter 11

Manipulators Come in All Sizes

"So, in the interests of survival, they trained themselves to be agreeing machines instead of thinking machines. All their minds had to do was to discover what other people were thinking, and then they thought that, too."

Kurt Vonnegut

There are manipulators of all ages out there. The youngest manipulator I ever met was four years old at the time, and happened to be my son Ivan. I was going out with some friends, and he asked me to stay home with him. "No, sweetheart, I will go out and you stay here with the babysitter. Your daddy will keep you company when he comes back from work." To which he answered, "Mom, if you really ... *really* loved me ... you wouldn't leave me here all alone." And then he pouted like he was going to start crying.

I felt this twisting guilty sensation in my gut, but then I thought to myself, "If I stay, I'll regret it, and I'm not doing him any favors ..." So I walked towards the door. Then he started crying and hung on to my leg. "Pleaaaaase Mom, don't leave me here all alone! Please, please, please, please ... I promise I'll be good, I'll do *anything*! But please! Don't *abandon* me!" (Sophisticated vocabulary for such a young age.)

His tears made me feel so sad, but I knew better. If I stayed, next time he'd know what he had to do to keep me from going out. So, simultaneously feeling like a terrible and a responsible mother, I left. The sitter had to pull his grip from my leg as I was gently pushing the door shut. I went downstairs feeling incredibly guilty and sad, since I could still hear his ferocious screaming through the door.

When I arrived at the restaurant, I couldn't resist it any more and I called home. Still feeling guilty, I wondered if I had made the right decision leaving him in such a desperate state. My mind knew that I did the right thing, but my heart was breaking. (Have I mentioned that mind and heart have a hard time communicating?)

When the sitter picked up the phone and I asked her how long Ivan cried for, she told me that after I left he went to his room, got his Yiya[17], (the teddy bear that has been an honorary member of this family for the last sixteen years), turned on the TV and watched a rerun of the Teletubbies while sucking his thumb.

I had my AHA! moment then. Things weren't as bad as I had thought. Actually, it felt AWESOME. I was so relieved that I had decided to call, because my mind had been creating pictures of Ivan crying nonstop like a madman and maybe the neighbors calling the police and the babysitter ready to jump out the window. But everything was all right.

17
I know that the right way is to say "hard of hearing." It's a little too complicated to change the picture. I apologize for any inconvenience.

If I had given in, a manipulator would have been created. Next time I went out, I witnessed a little bit of drama, but it was much less intense than the first time. The following time he avoided the drama completely and went directly to the TV with Yiya and his thumb. Problem solved.

Years later I witnessed a similar situation with one of my friends. I went to her house to pick her up, and the same little kiddo story that happened to me a few years before was happening to her.

"Mom, if you really loved me, you wouldn't leave me here all alone." I was appalled to hear my friend say, "Mommy loves you, sweetheart, and I know you will be all alone with the babysitter, but if *you let* mommy go out to her dinner, I will take you tomorrow to the toy store and get you any toy you like."

As we were leaving, I asked her why she'd caved in. She explained to me, "I need to do it because I don't want to damage the emotional health of my son." I learned later that the toy she got him was an $80 remote-control car. And the boy learned his lesson. He kept throwing fits, and the mom kept buying these kinds of gifts for the kiddo every time she went out.

I knew she felt guilty, but I understood the situation better. I also knew that it was her emotional health that was more at risk than the boy's. Many years have passed—twelve to be exact—and we are still friends, but from time to time, I see the monster she created.

He is a teenager now, and he is extremely rude to her. He bosses her around, insults her and makes fun of her in front of her friends, and she obviously doesn't know how to discipline him. He is otherwise a nice young man, who is polite toward everyone else, but he treats his mother like dirt. I can't help but wonder if this is the kind of emotional health she was referring to back then. When he was a child, his tears felt like punishment to the mother, and she didn't have the backbone to disappoint him. As a consequence, her son now walks all over her, and she doesn't know how to fix it.

Children who successfully manipulate their parents learn that manipulation is an effective way to get what they want. The little person grows up, but the manipulative methods remain.

Here's something else that happened to me: One day (years later) when I told Ivan to help clean the kitchen, he responded, "Is that why you wanted children? To have free labor?"

"Not only for that," I said, "but to do as you are told and to be nice to your little brother."

"OK," he replied, and went off to wash the dishes.

My other son, Fernando, on the other hand, never argued about chores. He actually loved vacuuming the carpet. I never figured out why.

Another dialog from one of my clients went like this:

"MOM! you yelled at me, I'm going to call 911 and they will lock you in jail for abusing the children in this household!" "Please call them, and when you are done, tell them that I also want to talk to them so I can tell the officer what you did ... Actually, on second thought, I'll call them for you and I'll let you talk to them."

The mom then rushed to the phone and brought it near the boy so he could see her dialing.

"NO, MOM NO! It's OK, I forgive you just this one time."

"No, darling, *I forgive you* this time. Next time you tell me that you will call the police because I yelled at you, I will be the first one to drive you to the police station so we can have a nice conversation with them."

When my clients become assertive, they crack me up with the creative ways they handle their children. But I won't say it's easy, since some children are strong-willed. We, as parents, need to be even stronger. I know it's hard, and sometimes it is easier to give up and let them have their way instead of dealing with another fight. As a mother, I know how tiring and emotionally draining it can be. In one case, after a very difficult day spent withstanding a series of temper tantrums from one of my sons, I went to bed feeling a strong pulsating sensation from the blood vessels in my temples. The next day, I woke up to find that a lot of my hair had turned gray. Was it worth it? Yes, it was. If I could've done it in a less stressful way, that would have been even better, but I didn't know a better approach. I just did the best I could, and I'm satisfied with how the boys have turned out.

I have seen several clients who still live with very manipulative mothers and are afraid to move out, go out, or speak up because their mom will use her illness (real or imaginary) to control them.

"Fine, go out, have fun, but if I get a headache like the ones I usually get, and if you are not here, I'll die for sure, and you'll carry that in your conscience, that you killed your poor old mother."

"Mom, please, you've been fine the last week, what are you talking about? Worse case you call 911 or call me and I'll come home right away."

"Just listening to you is giving me already a headache. You are a selfish child who only cares about yourself. Go! Don't let me keep you from enjoying yourself!"

So when you leave after a litany like that, you'll be thinking that maybe your mom's bad headache may lead to a stroke or imagine her on the floor with the paramedics breaking into the house to give her artificial respiration. Those thoughts won't let you enjoy that party you went to with your friends and will make you feel like a terrible son or daughter. That kind of mental influence is a powerful incentive to obey, because nobody wants to feel like that. You have to be aware that guilt affects the *I am* too.

Realize that if a tiny child is strong enough to walk to the TV, suck his thumb and enjoy an episode of Teletubbies, then believe me, your mother is not going to be foaming at the mouth like a sick dog as soon as you leave the house. She'll probably be on the phone with her friend checking out the next Bingo tournament.

Manipulators won't throw fits without an audience. Fits are tiring, and they need to save their energy to use when you get back. Of course, when you come back from the party she didn't want you going to, the manipulative parent will slip back into character and put on the act once more.

You will love this video, which shows exactly what I'm talking about. Go to YouTube and look for: Funny fuse faves: boy tantrum. (It's the video that lasts 2 minutes 11 seconds.)

Please remember that when you say "No" to your children and they look upset, they are putting on a show for you. Their feelings may be real, and their performance may be heartfelt, but it is still a performance, and it's not one that should be rewarded. This may be painful for you, and it will probably be painful to your child, but allowing them to learn the wrong lessons will only do them harm in the long run.

Manipulators aren't like that with everybody, they will only be manipulative with people they think it will work on. It won't work on everyone—more than one person will tell them off, and believe me, they'll be smart and stop. Be that person. Don't be like my friend who was afraid of hurting the emotional health of her little brat. Adults that manipulate others are people who are used to having their way with their parents, because they had weak-willed parents and they were strong-willed children.

Personal anecdote

I went to Catholic school all my childhood. One time in elementary school, when I was around seven or eight, I was sitting in one of the nuns' offices. I don't remember why I was there. There was another girl ahead of me, and I heard her comment on a pretty painting the nun had in her office. To my surprise, I saw the nun remove the painting from the wall and give it to the girl.

"You like it? It's yours," the nun said.

"Really?" the girl said.

"Sure thing, keep it."

I sat there, I observed and I learned. Then I scanned the room to see if there was something I liked. I found a little porcelain girl, with a beautiful green dress sitting on a shelf.

"Yes, that's the one I want," I thought. When I saw my chance, I commented to that same nun how much I liked that little porcelain girl. And just as I expected, the same thing as before happened.

"You like it? It's yours," she said.

"Oh Gosh, thank you!"

I played the *'Really? No way! You have to be kidding me'* role.

And she played her *'I insist'* role.

To my delight I left her office with a beautiful porcelain girl.

According to my memories of my childhood as a girl, I was an absolute angel. And yet, when the angel saw what she could get away with, she went right ahead and did it. If the nun had said "no" to the other girl, I would have never asked. That being said, if my mom hadn't banned me from going to the nun's office to get more stuff, I would have probably come back with a little trolley to see what else I could have gotten away with.

Some parents inadvertently train their children to throw fits to get what they want. The parent gives in, and the child learns a lesson. Even dogs know that if they bark, whine or yelp enough, their owners will usually give in to the dog's whims.

Cuco (pronounced coo-coh) was the dog that we had when I was in high school. Cuco was a bratty dog, but I believe that he was the happiest dog on the planet. He trained us well to let him get away with stuff. If we were in the dining room eating, Cuco would bug the heck out of us to receive a piece of our food. He would whine, cry, jump, bark, moan, lick and scratch our legs. And we, the supposed owners, growing tired of him being a brat, would give him a piece of chicken while commenting among ourselves, "What's wrong with this dog?" Now that I understand the dynamic between Cuco and our family at dinner time, the question should not have been "What's wrong with Cuco?" The real question was "What's wrong with us?"

The answer to that question is: ignorance. We didn't know any better.

There are children who behave like total brats with their grandparents and behave like angels with their parents, and vice versa. Why? Because their parents trained them to behave like angels and the grandparents let them behave like brats. For example, I was a brat with my paternal grandparents and an angel with my parents and maternal grandparents. Why? Because my parents didn't take any crap from me. If I had been raised by my paternal grandparents I would have been a completely different person.

We want to comply because we care

Manipulators exist when there is someone to be manipulated, but that someone must care enough to allow themselves to be manipulated. If a complete stranger knocked on your door and told you. "If you don't call me every day and tell me how much you love me, I'll be miserable for the rest of my life," you'd find it extremely easy to slam the door in their face while thinking "What's wrong with this person?" If he gave you the silent treatment, you would think "Why should I care?" If he started crying and told you how mean you were for not doing as he requested, you would think "Why does this guy keep bothering me?"

You'd find it easy to validate your feelings of 'I'm fine, he is wrong.' But strangers know that they cannot get their way with you, because there's no emotional leverage for them to take advantage of. Instead, they search for potential targets among their loved ones. And your loved ones won't search for strangers to comply with their requests; they know that they'd only get the door slammed in their faces. That's why they go to you. Are they dumb? No they are not. They are incredibly smart; they know who they can take advantage of. Unfortunately.

How can this information be useful?

We must acknowledge that we are all more prone to get away with things if somebody lets us, and somebody else can be more prone to want to get away with things if we let them. Don't be afraid of your manipulators, they usually shape up. Saying "No" won't break anyone. Everybody will be fine.

Chapter 12

Being Too Nice Can Hurt You

"A lot of people are afraid to tell the truth, to say no. That's where toughness comes into play. Toughness is not being a bully. It's having backbone."

Robert Kiyosaki

Did you know that, even when you think that you are a pushover, you eventually do speak up? We all do. It's not a matter of 'what' but a matter of 'when' and 'how.'

Let me tell a made-up story to illustrate my point. Let's pretend that you are a married woman with children and that you happen to have a friend named Bugs. Let's also assume that you tend to be nice because you don't like hurting people's feelings. (Like many of us.)

Day 1

You are in your house, it's about 4:30 PM and Bugs knocks on the door, because she happens to be in the neighborhood. Even though you are busy, you're happy to see her. She hangs out in the living room chitchatting with you. Although you have a list of things to do, you don't mind postponing them. Just before dinner, she leaves.

You are happy that she came by to visit, and you had a nice time, but you wish that she had called before she stopped by. Still, it's OK. You have a solid and intact friendship.

Day 2

The next day, Bugs knocks on your door again. Once more, she happened to be in the neighborhood. You open the door and let her in. This time, you're not as excited to see her as you were yesterday, but you still welcome her. This time, she doesn't leave before you serve dinner. Since you don't know what else to do, you invite her to join you, which she graciously accepts. When your husband comes home from work and sees her, he gives you this look that says, "She's here … again?" You can only shrug your shoulders and give him a look saying "I have no idea why she's here."

After dinner, she thanks you and leaves.

You feel somewhat annoyed and wonder why Bugs has chosen to visit you two days in a row. You don't speak up, because you want her to be your friend and are willing to make excuses for her: Maybe she's lonely, maybe she does have a lot of things to do in the neighborhood, and maybe that's what friends are supposed to do. Your friendship is still intact, even if it's showing little cracks.

Day 3

On the following day, you come home late after running errands. When you left, the kids were with a babysitter. However, you get home to find Bugs sitting with your kids in the family room watching TV, and they haven't done their homework. The kids are happy to see her, because she's funny and nice. You can't help but think, "What the hell is wrong with her?" Even so, you keep your composure, because she is your friend and you don't want to hurt her feelings. You (despite feeling furious) reason with yourself, "Well, the kids like her, and she is a good person." But you are also mad because the children would have done their homework had she not been there.

When you call the kids for dinner, they start begging you: "Please, mommy! We want *Aunty* Bugs to stay for dinner; we like her a lot." You are feeling annoyed by now, but you cannot make sense of your feelings. "Why am I getting pissed at Bugs?" you ask yourself.

She's nice, and of course, the kids like her, too. Well, you figure that sharing a little extra food with her won't hurt. Besides, Bugs doesn't eat much. While eating dinner, your husband comes home from work and gives you the same frown as before, and you return a similar look. Nobody says anything, because you both want to be polite and act like 'grown-ups.'

After dinner, you say you are tired, but instead of Bugs taking this hint and leaving, she stays and tells you to go to sleep and that she'll read books to the kids and tuck them into bed. You agree because you are tired, but one part of you is upset. Still, you reason with yourself, "Why am I furious? The kids like her, and it's so nice of her to offer to tuck the kids in bed and read them bedtime stories. She's giving me some time to rest because I'm tired."

Eventually, you hear Bugs leave at around 11PM, because after she tucked the kids in bed, she went to your family room and watched a movie. At this point, you are definitely feeling angry, and you are wondering if you want to be her friend any more. You don't say anything, but you have a hard time sleeping because you are really annoyed. You wonder if you have a reason to feel like that, but you feel that you don't like her any more.

Day 4

Next day, Bugs knocks on your door. Once again, she just happens to be in the neighborhood. This time when you open the door, you roll your eyes and say, "Now what?"

You are hoping that she gets the hint. Usually, whether unintentionally or deliberately, people with boundary issues are the last ones to pick up on hints. So, unsurprisingly, she does not get your point because you are not direct enough.

She tells you, "I was in the neighborhood and wanted to stop by for a little while if it's OK with you." You open the door, clearly mad, but don't say anything because you want to be polite. However, by now you don't care about her any more, and you are so annoyed that you hope to never see her again.

She spends the afternoon in the house, helping your children with their homework and, after dinner, watching TV with them. You and your husband discuss the situation and both of you are angry at her for having such nerve. The truth is that you are not angry at her; you are angry at yourselves for allowing it to happen. Still, you and your husband both decide to be prudent, to not say anything and to not let *her behavior bother you*. (As a matter of fact, feeling angry is the right thing to feel because she is flagrantly violating your boundaries.) But you still reason that the children are happy, and she is such a great help with them. In fact, you should be grateful.

You have a group of friends together, and you wonder whether pissing Bugs off will alienate you from the other friends in the group. After all, Bugs has been so kind to you. You shouldn't complain, right? You go to sleep furious as you hear Bugs tuck the children in bed. But, you want to throw up when you hear your daughter tell her: "I love you *Aunty* Bugs; you are so nice to me!" However, she doesn't leave, and you wonder what you should do next, while getting angrier and angrier.

Then, Bugs knocks on the door of your bedroom, wearing one of your pajamas that she found in the laundry room. She jumps in bed with you and your husband, and then she says to you: Good night!

At that moment you explode:

"Get the hell out of here; I hate you! I don't want to see you again! What's wrong with you! You are a freak; you are a moron! Give me my pajamas back, and if you ever happen to be in this neighborhood again, please don't knock on this door, or I'll call the police!"

Then, Bugs gets offended: "Why? I was just trying to help. I was trying to be a good friend to you. Please tell me what I have done to make you mad. Clearly, you are the one with a problem; look at you … all mad. I am calm. Who is the one with the problem?"

You scream: "Shut up and leave now, and never EVER COME BACK AGAIN!"

So, Bugs leaves, crying, but before she leaves, she goes to the kids' room, and tells them that she's leaving and wants to say good-bye. Bugs tells them that she loves them so much, and they love her and they cry "But why, Aunty Bugs; why are you leaving? We love you." Bugs replies "Because your mommy thinks that I'm a freak and a moron, and she says she hates me." Then the kids hate you. You go to bed furious, so mad that you cannot make sense of the situation, and you just swear that you don't want to see her again. EVER.

The End

And the moral of the story is

At some point in your life, after the pressure builds up enough, you *will* speak up, one way or another.

The problem is not the what, but the when and the how. The person in this story should have spoken up the moment that she felt a little bit of annoyance. Instead, she allowed Bugs to keep coming back and dig herself deeper and deeper into her home and her life. In more general terms, she let the situation escalate until she lost control of her reactions and responded aggressively.

As you can tell, the story didn't end well for *you* (thank you for being my guinea pig). It's true that *you* got rid of Bugs, but due to the nature of *your* reaction, *your* kids ended up thinking that their mother was the bad guy, and *you* went to bed angry and confused. If *you* had spoken up sooner or had set boundaries previously, things would have turned out very differently.

There are plenty of people who will push the envelope the way that Bugs did in this story, because people with boundary issues, like Bugs, either won't pick up on hints or will pretend not to notice them. Boundaries are necessary and are not meant to punish others, but to protect us from getting into uncomfortable situations we want to avoid.

People like Bugs enter our lives at times. Replace the name Bugs with words like son, coworker, mother-in-law, sister, aunt, or friend. Some of us have to deal with people who lack boundaries, and we can learn to prevent their overstepping our boundaries. Other people rarely or never have to deal with something like this until they get married, at which point they discover that the new extended family has boundary issues.

You now know that at some point you will have to speak up. Don't wait until you start showing stress-related illnesses like Irritable bowel syndrome, migraines, asthma or diabetes. But I have also read that long periods of stress mess up our immune system, which make us vulnerable to many illnesses, not just the ones I mentioned before.

Trust your gut feeling. That little voice, telling you that something's wrong. Listen to it. If someone is repeatedly making you feel embarrassed, angry, frustrated or generally uncomfortable, listen to the part of you that says to speak up! Don't try to make excuses for them and for you to not speak up. ("Because it's rude," or "Because it's inappropriate.")

Interesting fact: *People tell me that they want to speak up but they feel that they don't have a valid excuse. After any kind of boundary violation is endured, people feel that they have to have a complete and accurate list of 'violations', as though they were at the police station giving details of the crime. However, when you ask somebody to stop and they ask you why, you can simply say:*

"Because it doesn't feel right."

Hang on to that. That's all you need to do. Just the way you say it when you have a headache, "It doesn't feel right," and you are not going around explaining how your head feels or where.

Let's redo Day 3

Let's apply the previous discussion to the story of Bugs, exploring one way to handle Day 3 differently.

On Day 3, you come home late after running errands. When you left, the kids were with a babysitter. However, you come home to find Bugs sitting with your kids in the family room watching TV. The kids are happy to see her, because she is funny and nice. You start wondering "what the hell is wrong with her?" Even so, you keep your composure, because she is your friend, and you don't want to hurt her feelings. You (despite feeling furious) reason with yourself, "Well, the kids like her, and she is a good person."

However, it's clear to you that this cannot continue. You go to your room to think about the "how" (to kick her out) because you are already clear about the "what."

You consider what you are going to say, knowing that you need to be as firm as the situation requires. You are nervous and that is OK; you are not used to kicking people out of places.

In my experience, the "broken record" technique is what works best in situations like this. With the "broken record," people repeat the same point over and over again, without responding to any arguments. People with boundary issues can have AMAZING debating skills, and they will use those skills to negotiate their way around any rational arguments of yours. If you start a debating match, you are far more likely to lose, believe me. But poor debating skills don't mean that you have to put up with someone's behavior. Therefore, in these cases a very effective tactic is to first mirror what the other person is saying, and then repeat yourself.

You leave your room and tell Bugs:

"Bugs, I have thought about what I am about to say, and I want you to leave now."

"But why? What have I done to you?"

"Nothing. I would just prefer that you leave, please."

"But, why? Don't you see that I'm here to help?"

"Yes, I do, but I prefer that you go home."

"You are probably upset because you had a bad day at work. Go to sleep, dear I'll take care of the children."

"Yes, I probably am upset from work, but I would prefer that you return to your house now."

"You are getting personal, you know?" (Of course, you weren't, but remember that a discussion increases the odds of failure.) "Wait until your husband comes back from work so we can discuss it."

"I'm sure you feel that way, but I want you to go home now."

"But my house got foreclosed on ten minutes ago, and I have nowhere to go."

"I'm sorry about your house, but I would still like you to leave my house now."

"But I thought we were friends."

Remember: if they play the "we are friend and family card," don't fall for the temptation of explaining why you think that you are friends. If you do, you'll end up having to define for her what a friend is and why her definition of friend is not the same as yours; people like this are often expert debaters with a side dish of drama queen.

"Yes, you thought we were friends, but I want you to leave my house now."

"What are you saying? That we are not friends? What's wrong with you; you are so selfish!"

"I hear you, but I want you to leave my house now."

Suppose the children arrive and ask: "What's going on?"

"Your mommy is kicking me out."

And the children start defending her and begging you not to be rude.

"Mom! Don't be rude; let her stay!"

You ignore the kids and talk to Bugs again. (She wants to turn your family against you so you become the bad guy. Completely ignore the children no matter how much they scream and cry.)

"I want you to leave NOW," and you hold the door open for her to leave.

Bugs leaves while crying and telling you how much she loves you and your kids, and, of course, how much she's going to miss them.

You close the door and when your kids calm down, you talk to them about boundaries.

Sometimes life is spiced by drama. Learn to tackle it with your head held high. Who is pushing your buttons in your life? Ask yourself how long you will wait until you decide to speak up. When drama is unavoidable, BE THE ONE IN CHARGE. Don't play the role of the victim; if you have to choose between your sanity and your bully's sanity: choose your sanity.

Everyone is in charge of his or her own well-being. With some people, win-win approaches don't exist, and if you choose the "I lose, you win approach," you will lose respect for yourself and hurt your self-esteem. If, on the other hand, you do speak up, you realize that some drama will occur because someone is stepping over the line. Grab the drama, take control of the situation, and win.

So far this sounds reasonable. But when you speak up for the first time, you *will* feel very nervous, shaky and guilty. You might think that you're not a good person and wonder why you have to put up with so much stress in your life. We all go through that, believe me. The truth is that you are a good person, and speaking up makes you a better person, with self-respect and healthy boundaries.

The emotional shock that comes from speaking up to somebody you love or care about will last about two days. However, if it's someone you don't care about, but only have to put up with, the shock probably won't last ten minutes. After two days, you will feel better and realize that it was something you needed to do at some point. The good news is that the first time you assert yourself is the hardest. The bad news is that sometimes needy people are more resilient than cockroaches and they return to try imposing on you again and again and again.

When you reach the point at which speaking up becomes second nature to you, you will feel proud of yourself and you will like yourself better. You will realize that you are a person worth respecting.

Remember: You do have boundaries, and you know how to enforce them, but it's up to you to actually enforce those boundaries before you get too upset. When my clients feel completely powerless, I tell them the story of Bugs. Then they laugh and realize that life is full of people who are either givers or takers. Manipulators are takers, and they need to take things or impose their needs on others. The simplest solution is: don't volunteer for the position.

The ideal situation is always a win-win. But sometimes that's impossible with some people.

My clients tell me sometimes that their manipulators are givers.

"They give me compliments, shower me with gifts and generous birthday presents, they regularly send me cards telling me what a wonderful person I am, but then they impose on me, get mad if I don't invite them, call them, cater to them or if I happen to prefer somebody else."

"They are not givers, they are takers because their gifts are bribery." I respond.

"But then I feel bad if I don't call them, invite them, write them etc."

"You have to speak up and say 'no' if it feels right in your heart."

We all have a little voice inside ourselves that tells us what feels right and what feels wrong. And when it feels wrong, it says, "This doesn't feel right; do something about it." We tend to give more attention to our more physical feelings, because we assume that our physical feelings are "more real." However, our emotional feelings are just as important an indicator of our overall health as our physical feelings are.

When my clients, or people in general, focus their attention on doing what *looks* right instead of what *feels* right, they end up forgetting what they really want. I ask them what their goals are in life, what makes them smile and what they are passionate about and they give me this blank look and say, "Me? I have no idea." It's like they have forgotten that they are allowed to have goals.

You have to listen to that voice. If you don't, *it will eventually shut down, and you will forget who you are and what you want. You will end up being whatever others want you to be and you will want what others want you to want.* You will start second guessing everything that you want from life, from what you buy when you go shopping to what you order at a restaurant. Saying "yes" constantly without setting healthy boundaries will strengthen your "insecurity muscles." Instead, you need to exercise your "assertiveness muscles." Otherwise, when somebody pushes your buttons, you will wait until you are enraged or furious to do something about it.

As a hypnotherapist, I find it easy to convince my clients that there's nothing wrong with them when they tell me about their phobias, procrastination problems, self-sabotage, low self-esteem, etc. That's the easy part. They are usually willing to believe me, and they tend to understand the dynamics of the mind quite quickly.

The difficult part is to convince them that when they feel irritated or uncomfortable because someone oversteps their boundaries and infringes on their personal space and rights, it is not selfish for them to speak up. They often ask me, "Can you keep me from being bothered by my mother emotionally blackmailing me all the time? I want to do everything that I can to accommodate all her wishes, but I don't want to be annoyed at her or at myself." It's possible that I could do that, but it would be much harder, because it wouldn't solve the real problem: their inability to talk back. It would be similar to asking a doctor to help you deal with the pain of an infection, instead of treating the infection itself.

Anger builds up

Here is an extreme case that I heard of. When I lived in Saskatchewan, Canada, there was an old couple everybody knew. One day, when the couple came home and the husband opened the gate to get the car in, she didn't drive the car through the driveway but instead deliberately drove over her husband. Then she backed up and ran him over a few more times to make sure that he was dead. From what I remember hearing at the time, he had been abusive and bullying towards her throughout their marriage. This woman reached the point where she had enough and preferred to spend the rest of her life in jail rather than continue putting up with the ol' bastard.

Or consider the example of Harita. Her parents arranged her marriage without her consent and she gave in to be *a good daughter*. However, she had a dream of becoming a professional and didn't want to get married at all, let alone to the guy her parents picked out. Now her parents and in-laws are bugging her to give everybody a grandchild. Harita changed her life plans to please her parents, giving up the possibility of education, achievement and romance. Yet, even after all of those sacrifices, they continue to pester her to bend her life even further away from what she wanted. She was disgusted at them and she felt powerless.

With clients like her, I ask them to close their eyes and imagine the following (this is not a hypnosis, it is as simple as close your eyes and imagine):

"So, Harita, please close your eyes and imagine that your parents are in front of you and suddenly, through magic they start shrinking and they become ants. You get close to them and carefully pick them up … there … your parents are there, in your hand, like two little ants … Now, I want you to grab a tissue box that you just found, grab a little plate with water, grab some grass, and make a little house for your ants."

That's when she (and all the clients in similar situation) start frowning.

"Why are you frowning?" I ask.

"Because I don't want to put the damn ants in the tissue box, I want to throw them onto the floor and step on them."

"You can open your eyes now … You are telling me that you want to harm the ants."

(Eyes opened and talking to me normally) "Yes! I want to kill them! I hate them!"

"What if they haven't told you what to do and they would have been respectful of your decisions?"

"I wouldn't be mad at them."

"What if you had spoken up and refused to marry, refused to listen to their nonsense, refused to let them intrude."

"I wouldn't be mad at them."

"So, what would happen if we plan a way to have a conversation with your parents in which you make your boundaries clear?"

"That would be nice, scary but nice."

"Yes, it's scary, but those thoughts of killing the ants show me your pent up anger, and pent up anger in the long run is bad for your health."

If we don't speak up and assert ourselves at the right time, our chances of becoming ill are much higher. If Harita had told me that she didn't let her parents bother her and that she had forgiven them, then in the ant example, she would have safely kept the ants in the tissue box.

I have used the *"Imagine the manipulator as an ant"* exercise on many different clients. To my surprise, I'm still waiting to get a client who says he'll take care of the ants. Inevitably, they want to do something violent like smash, boil, burn or drown the poor, helpless little ants.

Some people will be angry at you for saying "no." However, if you say "yes" and agree to something which you truly do not want to do, you will be angry at yourself. Believe me, that doesn't feel good.

Dorothy, my cousin, is an HR Director at a Fortune 500 company in Mexico. She has a secretary who is very rude to her on a regular basis, and rolls her eyes at any request she makes. If Dorothy asks for a favor, Sammy says: "Don't you see that I'm busy with your darn report?" or "I'm leaving early today and I'm not coming in tomorrow."

"OK," Dorothy says, "but I still need you to finish the payroll report I asked you to do last week."

"Didn't you just hear what I just said? Or should I spell it out for you. I am leaving today early and I'm not coming to work tomorrow, if you want that report ready you better hurry up."

Then Dorothy calls me:

"Alba, help, is it normal that the secretary talks to me that way?"

"No it's not."

"Why is she like that? She should be nicer to her boss, right?"

"I guess she should."

"I wonder what's wrong with her ..."

"Why don't you tell her that with that attitude there will be consequences?"

"What? She's going to get really mad."

"But you can get mad too, right?"

"Well, yeah, but I won't go down to *her* level, she's just a secretary."

"But you still can talk to her."

"If I do she'll make a scandal. I don't want a scandal, I need to be the *'grown up.'*"

Her excuses for not speaking up change all the time.

I want to be promoted.

I don't want to have a scandal.

I want to be the one who's virtuous and nice.

I don't want to lose my job.

I don't want to create a reputation for being mean.

Those are her excuses, but they all boil down to a single reason: She is afraid of her secretary. And she's mad. When I asked her to imagine Sammy as a cute little helpless ant in the palm of her hand, she was happy to smash the ant with a baseball bat (imaginary, of course). I have a lot of clients like Dorothy and Harita, and what I do is first lighten things up by sharing the story of Bugs with them. They like it and they realize that if things go too far, they will speak up, but, by then they will be absolutely furious and ready to attack.

Then I work on their self-esteem. One thing that abusers do is hurt people's self-esteem. Why? Because feeling powerless and afraid makes their self-esteem shrink and that will bring more powerlessness and that will make them shrink even more and that will make them feel more powerless and so on.

Working on their self-esteem empowers them, and then we create a plan of action. And they live happily ever after … until they need to speak up again.

Interesting fact: Some clients ask me, what if I'm the needy one? What if I want my sister, friend or boyfriend to love me, like me or be more intimate with me more than they actually are? We are all needy in one regard, we all have somebody out there that we wished were closer to us that they are. I have a friend I really like hanging out with: she's fun, compassionate and has amazing conversations. If she'd let me I'd be her best friend and she'd be mine, she has allergies and when I invite her over I prepare food that she can eat. But she never reaches out to me, and she never invites me to her get-togethers, if I don't call her she couldn't care less. What to do in that case? Let go of the attachment and move on to greener pastures. I cannot make anyone like me more than they do, but my time is precious and it would be better to use it wisely with people who truly like me. It's a matter of take it or leave it.

I've experienced this phenomenon myself. My youngest son Fernando had always been a good kid, but when he was around six years old, he started being rude to me when we had company. He'd argue, snap, and try to get his way, knowing that I was polite enough not to make a dramatic scene in front of my friends. I didn't know what to do or how to handle the situation because he wasn't embarrassed about yelling at me in front of my guests. Telling him, "Please go to your room," never worked, because he would start defying me and yelling, "I am not going anywhere, and who do you think you are?" To which I would respond with, "Don't talk to me like that; I am your mom." And then he would escalate further, and say something like, "I talk to you the way I want because you are a lousy mom."

I could see my guests' heads moving back and forth as if they were watching a tennis match, while my face was blushing more and more from frustration and embarrassment. I ended up becoming so angry that I later needed to call a friend to vent. "Is this normal? Why isn't my son more grateful?" On one particular evening, I became so mad that I declared to myself that there was *no way* I was going to let him play that card on me again. But I had to have some sort of plan. I thought about it for a few days. And, suddenly ...

AHA! I found the perfect solution to my problem. Remember, complainers aren't only angry at their attackers, but are mainly angry at themselves for feeling powerless. So, I was obviously mad at myself for letting Fernando behave like that.

That evening I told him that I wanted to talk to him, and the dialog went like this:

"The other day when we had company, you embarrassed me with your behavior, and I didn't like it. I have thought about it, and the next time you embarrass me in front of my guests and do not do as you are told the first time I am going to embarrass you, too."

"What are you going to do?"

"You'll have to apologize to me in front of everybody."

"I could apologize to you in private."

"So, you embarrass me in public, and then you apologize in private? I don't think so."

"What if I don't want to?"

"Then, you will be getting the *Mom no* treatment for two days, and we'll see how you like it."

Let me define *mom no*. It was so simple and clever that I cherish the spark of inspiration that brought the idea into my mind. It means just what the name says: I say "no" to whatever the kid asks for, over a certain period of time. Usually, a day or two is enough.

"Mom, can we stop at the skateboard store?"

"No."

"Mom, can I show you this video on YouTube? It's really cool!"

"No."

"Mom, can I invite my friend over for a playdate this Friday?"

"No."

"Mom, can you get me applesauce when you go to the supermarket?"

"No."

"I don't like your food, can you please make Mac and Cheese for me for dinner?"

"No."

"MOM! What do you mean you are not driving me today to soccer practice?"

"If you can get a carpool, that's fine with me, but I'm not driving today."

On days when there isn't much to say 'no' to, I just let him tag along when I go to the grocery store or even worse ... Toys R Us! As we walk through every aisle, he'll want everything ... and I'll say "no," of course.

Also, I stop doing his laundry.

"Mom! I don't have any more socks in the drawer; could you do the laundry, please?"

"No."

In addition, he is not allowed to play videogames. Why? Because the TV is mine. He's not allowed to play with his phone either, because the Internet connection is mine, and I am the one who pays for the service.

One day, when I first exercised the *mom no* for one day, I realized how much I actually do for them and how I am taken for granted. *Mom no* also serves as a reminder of how much you actually do for your children every single day. After a good *mom no* day, believe me, next time you say *yes* to something, they will almost get on their knees thanking you. They will be overly appreciative and they will actually think you are the nicest parent on the planet.

So, if there's a punishment that gives my children the creeps, it is the *mom no*. If you have bratty children and you don't know what to do, use it. No need to yell, get mad, whine, complain, pout, and negotiate. Simply say no to everything (and wear earplugs, if you are sensitive to high pitched screams.) You will love it. I promise.

Now going back to Fernando acting up in front of my guests. The rule was: "You are rude to me in front of the guests; therefore, you have to apologize to me in front of them."

And he has to say it like he means it, because if he rolls his eyes while saying "Soooorry mom," he'll have to do it again until I find his apology to be sincere enough to be acceptable. If he refuses, then *mom no* is in order.

Remember: When you plan in advance what you are going to say or do and stick to your guns, your chances for success are really high.

The day came when the apology was due, and just like any other child out there, his goal was not to comply, but to test my limits. He did apologize in private, but when it came time to apologize in front of my friends, he was rude and refused to do it. Since he didn't follow the rule, I stuck to the *mom no* treatment for a couple of days. As expected, he soon started begging for another chance and said that he'd never do it again, that please, it is pure torture for him, and he's just an innocent, tender, little kid, pleeeeeaaaassseeee, mom, pleeeeaaaaassseeee!

It was very hard. I knew that I was hurting him, and I wanted to give in and show mercy, but I followed through with it, and the end result was that it worked.

The next time my friends came around, he actually gave me a very nice and meaningful public apology, after that ... there haven't been any more displays of disrespect. Just the opposite. Since then he's charming with the guests, chatty and helpful.

That's when you realize that not all hope is lost. Neither with your children nor with the people who step over your personal boundaries.

How can this information be useful?

Try the 'ant experiment' yourself. Think of the people who are a little abusive towards you as being like little ants that are under your care. Don't try to analyze or rationalize your response, just try to determine your instinctive reaction to it. If you feel that you can carefully place them in a box and put grass, sugar (or whatever ants eat) and water in it, then you are fine. If you don't care about the ants one way or another, then that's also fine. It means that you have forgiven the abusers to a certain extent, and that they no longer pose a negative influence on your emotions. But if you want to squash them, it's because you have a pent-up store of repressed anger. That's when you have to start speaking up, because that anger is bad for your health. And, truth be told, much of that anger is towards yourself.

Initially, it may be terrifying. It may be harder than anything you've ever done in your life. But you have to ask yourself one simple question: has being forgiving made me happy? You must take a stand, you are worth it. You are worth your weight in gold.

I want to mention something important though. There are people who have suffered abuse and have really truly forgiven and live a life of pure, peaceful bliss. When that's the case they lovingly take care of their ants.

Chapter 13

Reclaiming Your Space, Your Sanity, and Your Self-respect

"Fool me once, shame on you, Fool me twice... shame on me."

Unknown Author

When our self-esteem is low, we don't treat ourselves right, and we let others treat us poorly. When I start working on my clients' self-esteem, many of them tell me that they have a "special someone" who is in charge of making their lives miserable, and that they don't speak up because it's not the polite, grown-up, mature, nice, Christian or forgiving way to respond.

The goal of this chapter is to share stories of clients who needed to speak up, to see if you can relate and hopefully find methods that will work for you too. If you don't have anyone in your life who likes taking advantage of you, feel free to skip this chapter.

Anika's Story

Her goal after working on her self-esteem? To put space between herself and her in-laws.

Anika comes from India. She's been married to Nilesh for seven years. They have a six-year-old girl and a four-year-old boy. They moved to Silicon Valley because Nilesh works for a high-tech company. They are both engineers, but she doesn't have a work permit to work in the US, and therefore she's a full time mom. She has a nice relationship with Nilesh and feels happy now that her self-esteem is better, but she confesses:

"I need to become strong to prepare for a major battle."

She explains to me that her only major complaint is that, because her in-laws live in India, when they come to the US for a visit, they stay with them six months at a time (each year).

"Why shouldn't I let them stay for so long if they live so far away?" she asks with a sad face.

"How long would you like them to stay?"

"Two weeks a year at the most."

"Have you told them that?"

"No way! They would get really sad! I don't want to break their hearts, but I don't like having them in my house for so long."

"And you would feel guilty?"

"Yes, but my mother-in-law is not nice to me, she is always telling me that I do everything wrong. She takes over the kitchen because I don't cook as well as her. Sometimes she makes nasty comments like: 'The good thing about having a daughter is that her children are my grandchildren for sure, with a son I will never know ... implying that my kids could have another dad. She also tells me that I stole *her baby* (Nilesh) from her."

As the conversation went on, I realized that not only were the in-laws in her house for six months in a row, but also her mother-in-law bugged her and put her down all the time.

"Have you talked to Nilesh about that?"

"Yes, but he just tells me not to let that bother me, that I should understand that he is an only child, that his parent's don't have a life and that they love the grandchildren so much, that we don't have the right to take *their grandchildren* away from them."

"Now they are *their* grandchildren, not the milkman's mother."

"Apparently so," she laughs,

"What if you talk to them?"

"Oh God! That would be hard. First because I'm terrified of her, second because she is so evil that she will manipulate the whole thing, she will scream, cry, blame and influence Nilesh, she's a horrible person indeed."

Then I said the following to catch her off-guard and make a paradigm shift.

"How could you not realize that they are only here to help, why would *YOU* (aka, the one with the problem) be annoyed, what's wrong with you, the kids love having their grandparents there, your husband will be taken care of better, the teachers love it when they go to the school meetings, your friends love it when they meet them, and you even love it when you are taking a shower, and they come in and rub your back with a brush."

"What?" Anika said, surprised, "Rubbing my back with a brush? In the shower? Over my dead body!"

"Exactly!" I nodded. "What kind of creep gets in the shower with their daughter-in-law to brush her back? You know that would be a major boundary issue, right? You wouldn't let them do that to you; you would think *'Gosh!, what's wrong with these people?'* and you would do something about it! You wouldn't second-guess yourself, would you? Well, having them stay so long when you don't want them to is a boundary violation as bad as the one with the shower. They're moving into your home for months on end without thinking about what you want, imposing and taking advantage of you. How is that not as bad as having them join you in the shower? You have to do something about it as strongly and firmly as you would if they wanted to join you to rub your naked back. Don't second-guess yourself. Trust your feelings, the same way you would trust your physical pain that is telling you to move your finger from an outlet before it starts having smoke coming out of it.

After practicing and role playing with her for weeks, this is what happened:

Anika had this conversation with her husband and got inspired with the "rubbing-the-back example." It gave her a clever idea.

"I want your parents to stay here for only two weeks a year only," Anika told her husband.

"Why? You know how my mother is, and she'll cry if we do that to her," her husband replied.

"Then, I want you to have sex with my mother."

"What? Are you crazy? Why should I do that?"

"Because she doesn't have a sex life and she'll cry if you don't have sex with her."

"Now you are making fun of me because that's completely different."

"Do you know how much it bugs me when they stay for so long? If you knew how miserable I am, if you know how annoyed I get when she comes to *my home* to patronize everyone and everything … well, I was thinking that the only thing comparable to that was for me to ask you to have sex with my mom."

"Well, I won't do it. Period."

"But my mom will cry! You don't want my mother to cry, do you?"

"I don't care if she cries or not; it's a matter of principle and I am not having sex with her."

"Exactly! I have my own dignity and principles, and allowing your parents to stay here for more than two weeks a year violates both of those. My parents don't stay more than two weeks a year here. They have a life; they don't want to be a nuisance."

"You see? That's the difference. I'm an only child, and they don't have a life because I am their life."

"Well then, it's about time that they start creating one, isn't it? I am nobody's aspirin, and I shouldn't be expected to supply them with a life just because they have chosen not to have one of their own."

"But it isn't their fault, because they don't know how to be independent; they are devoted parents, and they love us very much."

At this point Anika was getting tired of the discussion, and decided to simply use the broken record technique.

"This is my house too, isn't it? Well, I don't plan to let your parents stay here more than two weeks per year. Are you going to tell them that or should I?"

"You? They are going to hate you forever."

(Not engaging in the discussion) "I know they will. So, are you going to tell them that I don't want them here more than two weeks a year, or should I do it?"

"Can you be reasonable? You are being unreasonable."

"I'm sure you think I'm unreasonable. Are you going to tell them that I don't want them here more than two weeks a year or should I?"

Nilesh is weak and he couldn't deal with his strong willed mom, and now that Anika was taking a strong position, he tried leaving the room because he couldn't deal with the pressure. That's why, in the past, he stayed in a spectator's position, simply watching both women drive each other crazy for six months.

"If you leave the room, I assume you don't want to take care of this problem, which then becomes my problem; therefore, I'll grab the phone right now and call your parents in Bangalore."

"But, it's midnight there."

"I don't care."

"If you call them, there will be strong consequences."

"If you don't make up your mind about who is going to tell them about staying two weeks a year, there will be strong consequences as well."

"Really? Like what?"

"Like I'm going to be the one calling them, whether you want me to or not."

"But I want to see them often; they are my parents. I love them."

"Then fly to India and spend all your vacation with them."

"But I also want to be with you."

"Then you have to make up your mind, because your parents aren't staying here for more than two weeks each year as long as I have any say in the matter."

"Okay, I'll think of something that works out for everybody, but in the meantime, let's not do anything."

"I'm sure you'll think of something, and you will find ways to be with your parents in a different place than here, and I am very happy about that. Still, you haven't told me who's going to tell them that they cannot stay more than two weeks a year in this house."

"I'll tell them."

"Good. When are you going to tell them?"

"Tomorrow morning."

"Good. Just so you know, if by tomorrow night you haven't called them, I'll be the one making the phone call."

We planned this dialog on paper, and we did role playing, and even though she sounded confident, she was shaking inside. She didn't think that she'd actually dare to be that articulate when the time came, but it helped her to write the arguments down on paper. That way, she somewhat knew how the conversation was going to flow.

She was nervous all throughout the next day, and of course, Nilesh didn't call his parents. He just waited and hoped that Anika would change her mind.

The day after that, she asked, "Did you call your parents?"

"No, I thought we'd talk about it again" he replied.

"That wasn't part of the deal." After saying that, she went to her bedroom, locked the door and dialed India.

His mom answered the phone, and after getting through all the greetings, Anika said, "Mom, I have to tell you that this past visit was too long for me. I've been thinking about it, and I have decided that I would like you to visit us for only two weeks each year."

After getting over the shock, her mother-in-law started crying, blaming, explaining, and feeling sorry for herself. Anika confessed afterwards that the silences were the most uncomfortable parts of the conversation that she had to experience. Finally, her mother-in-law said, "You cannot make that decision yourself."

"Yes, I can, because this is my house," Anika responded.

"What does Nilesh say about it? You are a selfish girl after all we've done for you. Because you can't say that we don't help; we do help, a lot."

"You can ask Nilesh about it if you want, because I believe that you think I'm selfish and ungrateful; and yes, you do help a lot. But from now on, you are allowed in our house only two weeks a year."

"You don't have the right to tell us what to do."

"In my house I do."

"Well, let's see about that."

Nobody talked about the situation for months, and when Nilesh talked to his parents on the phone, Anika refused to talk since it also bugged her that she has to talk on the phone or Skype with her in-laws at least twice a week. She had decided to follow her heart in that matter, too. The following year, the in-laws bought tickets to come to the US for three months. Nobody asked Anika, and her husband was happy to share the news.

"They are compromising! Isn't that wonderful?"

"Where are they going after they've stayed here for two weeks?" Anika asked.

"What are you talking about?" Nilesh asked, playing dumb.

"You know what I'm talking about."

"Why are you so unreasonable?"

"Where are they going after they stay here for two weeks?"

"They are going to stay here three months, take it or leave it."

"Ok, I'll leave it. I'm going to talk to a lawyer about my rights, because if they stay, the kids and I are moving somewhere else until they leave. If you want them here, then fine, but I don't want them under the same roof as me. Your mom bugs me, she snoops, she gives advice, she criticizes the way I do things, she gives candy to the kids when I ask her not to, she takes possession of the house as if it were hers. So since I can't share a house with your parents for more than two weeks, I'll look for another place to stay."

"I'll tell her to be nice to you."

"That's not negotiable, and besides, you go to work all day, and sometimes you even travel. I'm the one who gets stuck dealing with them 24/7. I don't think so."

In the end, his parents came, stayed at Anika's house for only two weeks, and rented a condo afterwards. If Nilesh wanted to see them after work, he'd visit with the children. To Anika's surprise, her oldest daughter told her how relieved she was that her grandparents had left so soon, because her grandma had been criticizing her all the time and telling her things like, 'You are a selfish girl just like your mother.' Anika hadn't realized that her mother-in-law had been bugging not only her, but her daughter as well. She was even more reassured that she'd done the right thing.

Nilesh accepted Anika's rules, and when her in-laws were there for just two weeks, she was able to treat them really nicely, without reservations. She felt empowered after taking a stand on her ground. And empowered people are happy people.

EMPOWERED PEOPLE ARE HAPPY PEOPLE

Darling's Story

Her goal after achieving strong self-esteem was to have a loving family. Then we realized that we had to tweak the goal into: learning to say no to her brothers and look for a loving 'maybe adopted family' somewhere else.

Darling is a young single mother who told me about the hardships of her childhood. Her dad always called her mom 'trash'; the older siblings were dad's pride because they were boys, but Darling, being a girl, was as 'trashy' as mom and was effectively raised to be slave labor for her father and brothers.

When we met, she told me that she had no contact with her dad at all, and her brothers wanted nothing to do with her unless they needed money. She'd lend them money and then never hear from them again. Her mom had passed on.

"All I want is to have a family," she told me, "a family that, at Thanksgiving, sits together and enjoys a nice meal together. I don't have that family feeling, I feel isolated, and I desperately want them to love me."

That was the reason she gave me for lending her brothers money, even when she knew that they wouldn't do anything for her and that she'd never see that money again. She would regularly compromise her own well-being out of longing for a loving family, and as a consequence, she couldn't refuse her family because she still hoped that one day they would love her back. It was my duty to break her heart and tell her that the reconciliation she was hoping for was just not going to happen. If her brothers wanted nothing to do with her when things were going well for them, and they only called her when they needed money, odds were that they wouldn't become the loving family she was hoping for.

In Darling's case, her actual priority should have been her nine-year-old daughter Emily, but thanks to the years of abuse as a child, she saw her brothers as being intimidating, while her daughter was not. Since she was not intimidated by her daughter, she sacrificed time and money that should have been devoted to her girl in order to please her brothers. Saying yes to her brothers meant saying no to herself and to her daughter.

WHEN YOU SAY YES TO SOMETHING BECAUSE YOU ARE AFRAID OF SAYING NO, YOU HAVE TO REALIZE THAT YOU ARE ALSO SAYING NO TO SOMETHING ELSE THAT PROBABLY IS MORE IMPORTANT TO YOU

For years, Darling saved money to buy a condo for her and Emily. However, while she was saving this money, she had to rent a room in a house. Nobody wanted to rent out a room to her since she had a child, but she begged her landlord and promised them that her daughter wouldn't be a problem and that they would never notice her. Therefore, after picking her daughter from school she'd run errands, go to the public library or stay at Target's cafeteria until it was nighttime and time to sleep.

By the time we met, Darling had finally saved enough for the condo, but for some reason, she was holding off on making the actual purchase.

"If you have enough money to buy a condo, why don't you do it?" was my question.

"Because my brother wants to borrow that money from me," she responded.

"Who told him that you had that money?" I asked.

"I did." (we are not logical creatures, are we?)

In Darling's mind, she was being a good sister by *lending* that money to her brother instead of buying the condo. But that behavior showed her daughter that Darling valued her brothers' needs more highly than hers and the girl's. That was sending Emily the message "your needs are not important." That made Darling realize that the last thing she wanted was to see Emily become an adult with low self-esteem who doesn't know how to speak up because nobody taught her how to be assertive. If the daughter saw that the mother didn't speak up, the daughter wouldn't learn to speak up for herself. She would learn the lesson very well, even if it was the wrong lesson. That's when Darling realized how important it was to prioritize taking care of herself and her daughter and to let Emily see her doing so.

She also realized that there were a lot of people who loved her and were nice and supportive, but these people weren't to be found among her family. Rather, they were what I'd call a "sunshine committee," namely people in Darling's life who were kind, nice, encouraging, positive, and caring. She realized that she had the right to decide how nice she wanted to be to her brother, and that it was not being selfish not to give it to him.

In the end, Darling's goals were clear:

1. To say no to her brothers.
2. To show Emily that she valued her.
3. To buy the condo.

We practiced a dialog, and when the time came, she did amazingly well. Here it is:

"Hi, sister, I need money."

"Hi. I know you do, but this time I won't lend it to you."

"What? Why not? I am your brother."

"You are only my brother when you need something from me, and besides, you never pay me back."

"BUT I PROMISE YOU THAT I WILL PAY YOU BACK; WHAT KIND OF PERSON DO YOU THINK I AM?" He shouted, since he knew that shouting intimidated Darling and that made everything easier for him.

She was intimidated but remained firm. Besides it was only a phone call. When Darling realized that she was getting into a debate contest, which she'd probably lose, she decided to use the broken record technique and another technique that she was happy to share with me: 'the silence technique.'

She didn't know if she read about it in a book or if she came up with it by herself. My clients are amazing, and they can get creative when they feel empowered.

"What I think of you doesn't really matter right now, because I am not going to lend you money this time."

Then he tried pleading ... "But, I really need it sis, believe me; I wouldn't be bothering you if it wasn't really important."

[...silence...]

"Are you there?"

"Yes, I'm here."

"When can I come and get the money I need?"

"I'm not going to lend you money this time."

"But, why not! I am your brother! We are family, and we are supposed to help each other!"

[...silence...]

"Are you there?"

"Yes, I'm here."

"Could you please lend me the money?"

"No, and I have to go; please don't call me again."

"But you HAVE TO HELP ME!"

"Actually, I don't. Goodbye."

And that was it; as things turned out, she never heard from her brother again. She told me later that it hurt that he broke contact, but the truth is that there weren't any ties to start with. What she had was a bully-bullied relationship. Saying good-bye hurts, no matter what, like a splinter, but we have to do it at some point or another in our lives.

In the end, things worked out for her. She moved to her condo which she and her daughter both love, spends time with new friends, and takes care of both herself and her daughter.

Bruce's Story

His goal: to have peace of mind.

Bruce, a guy in his late 30's, loving father, loving husband, loving son, responsible employee but with stress levels that were off the charts. He constantly felt pressure to make everybody happy. It was his way of showing them how much he cared. The problem was that everybody in his family wanted different and sometimes conflicting things, so when he said 'yes' to one person's request, he was saying 'no' to somebody else.

He, like Dorothy, really believed that accommodating everybody's needs without considering his own made him virtuous, but the truth is that he didn't know how to say no without feeling guilty. A demanding family and Bruce's lack of backbone were the perfect combination to create a highly stressed and drained young man. He thought that making everybody happy was a great virtue, and there's nothing wrong with that. But in his case, that virtue defied common sense.

For example, his mom wanted him to visit every day, and she also wanted his wife to call her every day, since she was a widow and was very lonely. However, Bruce's wife didn't want to call her mother-in-law every day; which made his mom complain to him on a regular basis. His mom complained about his wife and his wife complained about his mom. They both expected him to decide who he loved more and who was right. And he thought it was his duty to be both women's mediator. His wife also wanted him to come home early from work because she needed a break from looking after their toddler. If he saw his mom after work, his wife would be upset, but if he came home directly from work, his mom would start a pity party.

Then there was Bruce's unemployed brother, Rich, who wanted Bruce to start a business with him. Bruce had already said yes, and Rich was pushing Bruce to quit his current job because Rich was running low on funds. Bruce had said yes, but the truth was that he didn't want to quit his job and start a business. He just felt it was his duty to help his brother.

At work, he also had a hard time keeping everybody happy. He had found a position in another area that he loved and which fit his skill set perfectly, they were even willing to pay him more than he received at his current job. They had made him an offer, and were just waiting for him to say yes. He was happy about that, but at the same time, he didn't want to hurt his current boss's feelings. Bruce's boss kept saying that he needed him to stay where he was, and that he was very disappointed that Bruce wanted to move to another area. He even promised that, in the near future, he'd try to match the other job's financial offer. In any case, the new job wanted Bruce to start ASAP, but his current boss wouldn't let go. He felt he had a duty to remain in his current position to please his boss.

In order to fulfill his mother's expectations, he had to disappoint his wife, but in order for him to fulfill his wife's expectations, he had to disappoint his brother and his mom. In order for him to fulfill his brother's expectations, he had to disappoint his boss and his wife. It wasn't any surprise that fatigue was etched in his face as he told me, "It's so hard to keep everybody happy."

"What makes you think you are in charge of everybody's happiness?" I asked.

His eyes almost popped out of his head as he looked at me with a 'What's wrong with you, lady?' expression on his face.

"Well, my mom is a widow, and she needs me. My wife is tired with the baby, so she needs me. My brother doesn't have a job, so he needs me. My boss needs me, too."

"Have you ever stopped and thought about what makes you happy?"

"*My* happiness comes from making my family happy."

"Are you happy?" I asked.

"No"

"Why not? You just said that your happiness comes from making others happy."

"Yes, but I can't make everybody happy at the same time, because there are conflicts of interests everywhere"

"Then you aren't happy. Are they happy?"

"No"

You need to be happy and kind to yourself. If your glass is not full, you can't share your happiness with others, because you cannot give what you don't have. The genuinely happiest people I know are people who know how to set boundaries.

We all know at least one special person who is always happy and cheerful. This person has the magical ability to make everything better just by being there. We enjoy their company, and thinking about them brings a smile to our faces. They will never say anything to hurt our feelings, but in fact do just the opposite, because they always have kind words for everyone around them.

They also don't make demands. If they see you once a week, they are happy; if they see you once a year, they are happy; if they see you once every five years, they are happy. They are not needy and don't wish you loved them more, that you wrote more often, or that you called more often. They are happy because they are their own best friend. Those people are a joy to be around. People who allow others to cross their boundaries are not the happiest people in the world because they start building up resentment.

We all know a happy wonderful person like that, despite how rare they are. For me, that person is my aunt Vero. She's always happy, and she's always making others around her very happy as well. She makes everybody feel special and loved. Many times I ask my clients to tell me about this special person they know who somehow manages to bring love and happiness to everyone around them. All of them can think of one of that special someone, and they all say, "Yes, I know someone like that."

"When was the last time you saw them?"

"About ten years ago. They were my friend in high school."

"If you interact with a lot of people every day, including your family, friends, and co-workers, then why do you have to come up with someone you haven't seen in ages?"

"It's because I've never known anybody else who was as happy and kind as that person."

The fact that all of my clients can think of one of these special people is one of the most interesting things about them. And often, that person is someone that they haven't seen in a long time. But despite this, the memories of those people stay in their hearts. It's very likely that those people made it their number-one priority to be happy, and without them ever realizing, they became a gift to the world. People like them have healthy boundaries and a healthy self-esteem, then, and when they share their love they do it from the bottom of their hearts and not because they want something in return.

HAPPY PEOPLE HAVE HEALTHY BOUNDARIES AND HEALTHY SELF-ESTEEM, THEN, AND WHEN THEY SHARE THEIR LOVE THEY DO IT FROM THE BOTTOM OF THEIR HEARTS, AND NOT BECAUSE THEY WANT SOMETHING IN RETURN

Now talking to Bruce:

"If I asked your mom, your brother, and your wife who was the kindest person they know, would they say that it was you?"

"No. I tend to be grouchy. But our grandpa was one of those 'happy people' you described. He never made people's problems into his, but still, he had a joyful mood to share with everybody, and we all loved being around him."

"Did he set boundaries?" I continued.

"Yes, his afternoon nap was sacred, and he let everybody know how important it was for him to take his nap."

"Did you feel offended that he needed to take a nap instead of being with you?"

"No, because when he was with us, he was happy and loving."

"What would he have done if you had asked him not to take his nap because you 'needed' him?"

"He would have laughed, and said yes … but after his nap. He was always laughing, even when he said 'no.'"

"I think it's easier for you to become that type of person than to be everybody's problem solver. Realistically, you cannot give what you don't have, and people around you should not expect you to fix their lives and dance to their tune because everybody has a different tune. You should create your own and dance that."

Bruce, the poor guy, wanted to please his mom, his brother, his wife and his boss at the same time. Sometimes, in fact most of the time, people cannot satisfy everybody. Therefore, it's best to start by satisfying yourself. After Bruce finally realized that it felt good to follow his heart and set limits, we started working on the best way to get there with the least amount of drama. To summarize weeks of work, this is what he did:

Regarding the situation with his mom, who wanted him to visit every day after work, he decided he wanted to have dinner with his mom once a week, and that the best day for him to visit was Thursday night. The rest of the week, he'd go home to his family instead. That made him happy, too, because he loved playing with his toddler before bedtime.

"What do you mean you won't come after work like you used to?" his mom asked when she heard about his decision.

"Exactly that; I can come on Thursdays for dinner, if you'd like me to join you."

"But, I am dying, and ever since you got married, you don't care about your poor old dying mom."

"I hear what you're saying, but I can only come on Thursdays for dinner, if that's OK with you."

"You never used to have that big mouth; you were such a good boy as a child. I'm sure that wife of yours is predisposing you against your poor, old, dying, sick mom, who's all alone."

He didn't get into a debate contest about his wife and about his mother's health, which was actually very good. Instead, he continued …

"I hear what you're saying, but I can only come on Thursdays. And if you ever badmouth my wife in front of me, I'm going to leave."

There was more drama, pouting, and complaining. But in the end, Bruce stuck to his guns, and his mom ended up saying, "I guess there's no way to make you change your mind. I'll see you on Thursday, then."

"See you on Thursday, and thank you for understanding."

Next, Bruce dealt with his brother.

"I know you don't have a job, but I don't want to quit my job to start a business with you."

"What do you mean, you don't want to? What about helping each other? What about me and my children? Are you going to let us starve?"

"No, you are smart, and you will figure it out. But I don't want to quit my job to start a business."

"But I need this! We need this! I thought you agreed already!"

Once again, Bruce didn't try to debate the point, but continued by saying, "I know I told you I would, but I said it because I was weak, not because I really wanted to do it."

"You are the most selfish person I know."

"I'm sure you feel that way."

"How are you going to feel if debt collectors come after us and our house gets foreclosed?"

"I'll feel really bad for you, but I am not going to quit my job."

"Fine! Suit yourself."

Obviously, the brother didn't like it. But, he managed.

And finally, Bruce faced his boss.

"What do you mean that you are moving to the other team? What about me?"

"I understand how you feel, but they won't wait for me forever, and I'm really interested in that position."

"That's so unfair, you know? I've been like a father to you."

"I know, and I am very grateful to you for that; still, I am giving you my two weeks' notice."

"Think it over; I will make you grow here." (He'd promised that in the past, but never happened) "The company is growing, and you have a great future here." (He'd said that in the past, too)

"I know you will, but I've made up my mind, and I am giving you my two-week notice."

"Is there anything I can do to make you change your mind?"

"No, there isn't."

"I guess that's it, then."

"Yes, that's it."

After each of these conversations, Bruce felt guilty for a couple of days. But he knew he was doing the right thing, and he also felt like a huge burden was lifted off his back.

Interesting fact: *Let me change my hat right now and move from hypnotherapist to career consultant. I have regular clients from Mexico who hire me for career advice. I have been doing it since 1996. I get to hear their professional life from beginning to end. There is something that I have never heard and I have to share it with you, in case it's helpful.*

When you resign your job or you want to move to another area because in the new area (or job) you will get more money, more vacation, more stock grants, more whatever ... and your boss tells you this ... 'Please don't go, here your possibilities for growth are incredibly high and I can promise that in about six months you will take so-and-so' job, and we'll double your salary, and we'll give you this and that.'

It will never happen. If he doesn't do it on the spot, with a signed firm offer, it will never ever happen. I have seen these kinds of situations more often than I can remember. And I'm not talking about little mom and pop stores with five employees. I'm talking about serious corporations with headquarters in the US. If it's not in writing, it will never happen. No matter how much you like, know and trust your boss. I told Bruce this and I tell you now.

*   *   *

Some clients, when I tell them to beware of loved ones who expect so much from them, will ask naively "But what if I am the one who is wrong because I am overly sensitive and overreacting?" My answer to that? Honor your overly sensitive and over reactive self, *and do something about it.* That overly sensitive you is wiser than you think, and you have to start trusting its intuition. If you have overly sensitive skin, you put on skin cream. If you have an overly sensitive digestive system, you watch what you eat (I hope). If you have overly sensitive teeth, you use a gentle toothpaste. But, when it comes to matters of feelings and the mind ... we second-guess ourselves and feel angry about being so sensitive.

If your mom is ill, and she asks you to please come see her right now, you will drop everything you are doing to go and check on her, but we all have a sixth sense that knows when it's manipulation instead of being real. If its manipulation, your mom will call you to drop everything for her every two weeks and when you check on her she will be just fine. If it's real, the calls won't be so frequent.

When someone is trying to manipulate you or take advantage of you, you don't just drop everything and go. You debate the situation inside your mind, thinking "I don't want to do it, but I should because she'll be mad if I don't ... but I don't want to do it because she only calls me when she needs something ... but I shouldn't be sensitive, she has a complicated life ... but I don't want to do it ... but she'll make me feel bad if I don't and then if I need something she won't be there for me ... wait a minute ... she's never there for me because she always says she's busy ... but I don't want to do it ... but I don't want her to get pissed and threaten me ... but I'll feel guilty if I don't and she'll keep on asking what I have to do that's more important than her ..." and this dialog goes on and on *ad-nauseum*.

I know exactly which clients say yes to manipulation, even before they say anything about it. To prove it, at some point in a matter-of-fact way I just say:

"You know, some people have this situation in their lives, and it makes them miserable. They are surrounded by people who manipulate them ... and the problem with that is that they go on and on with mental debates like ..." (like the one I described above).

When I do that I see my client's eyes get bigger and bigger in astonishment until they finally interrupt me and tell me: "THAT'S EXACTLY WHAT HAPPENS TO ME! YOU HAVE TO BE SOME SORT MIND READER!"

I deny that I'm a mind reader and I just blame it on pure coincidence. But I'm lying. I don't want them to know what I know:

That people who frequently go through those mental debates look emaciated and the bags under their eyes go all the way down to their throats.

Javier's Story

Javier was a high school teacher in his first full-time position. His problem was that he felt like he was too young. In fact, at the time, he could have passed for one of his own students. As the finals for his class approached, he panicked. His main fear was that a student might challenge him about a bad grade.

"Having to explain why I gave this kid a C+ makes me very nervous, and I don't even know what to say," he said. "They are so confident that they deserve an A+, and they'll argue until I feel completely drained. That situation really makes me tense."

"What makes you think that *you* have to explain yourself?" I asked.

"Well, he's there to ask me why I gave him a C+."

"Why don't you make him explain to you why he thinks he deserves an A—I suggested—giving the problem back to him. Think of the problem as being like a ball, and the one holding it has to give the explanation. If you ask him, 'Why would you give yourself an A in this exam?' the ball goes back to him, and he's the one who has to do the explaining."

"But, what if after that, he tells me why he thinks he deserves an A? You know, some of these kids can be very eloquent, and they win debate contests and all."

"First of all, realize that you are not in a debate contest; so if the kid says something like, 'This answer is complete, and this one is short, but clear, so I want you to give me an A,' then you simply have to respond, 'The answers are not good enough, and I'll leave the C; next time I want more details.' You are the teacher, after all."

"'But, that is not fair.' The student will say."

"On the contrary, it's perfectly fair."

"Now, if you think his explanation is good enough, change the grade. If his explanation isn't good enough, then don't. Set your boundaries, and don't let your students move you outside them. Don't grab the ball and let him make you explain yourself of what is fair and what isn't; just acknowledge his feelings. Say something like, 'I'm sorry you feel that way, but next time you'll do better, I'm sure.'"

"What if they call me a terrible teacher?"

"Then they're wrong. Your responsibility isn't to give them the grades they want, but to give them the grades they deserve. If you let your students dictate your boundaries, that would be bad teaching."

Maria

Her goal after having a better self-esteem: to break free from her mother's control.

For all of Maria's life, she had been manipulated by her mother. She was practically her mother's slave. Her mom's method of controlling her was to threaten to commit suicide. She believed her mom was serious because she had committed "half" suicides in the past, like slightly cutting her arms with a razor blade or taking a few sleeping pills to get ill enough to end up in the hospital, but never to the point of getting near dying. Maria always complied because she said she couldn't bear the thought that her mom's death would be her fault or that her entire family would hate her for it. As a result, she was in her thirties and still living with her mother. Her mom didn't know Maria had a boyfriend, Robert, because she banned her from dating.

By the time I met her, Maria was getting physically ill from the anger towards her mom that had accumulated throughout the years. She was a very nice and kind person, but she believed that she didn't have a choice and that her mom was her cross for her to bear. Still, Maria had a good career, was doing well financially, and she didn't want to live in her mom's house any more. Also, she wanted to marry her boyfriend.

We practiced and role played until she was ready.

"I prepared for the final fight with my mom. I found a place to live, not too far from her. I wasn't ready to move far away yet, but still, this was a huge step. I went to my room and packed my things, not letting mom know what I was doing; she thought I was organizing my room. I opened the door with my suitcases full, with an apartment waiting for me, and decided to start my new life. But first I had to deal with my mom's suicidal conversations."

"Mom, I'm leaving you; I found an apartment not too far from here, and I already paid the deposit, so I'm moving today. I'll come and visit often, you are still my mom and I love you, but living here is making me ill."

"If you leave, I'll die for sure."

"You probably will."

"I can't be alone, and you know it; there is no reason for me to live now."

"I thank you for all you've done for me, and I plan to do the same for my children."

"Children? What children? Are you having sex with somebody? Just what I needed to hear! Please go! And never come back! Don't even bother burying me." (She chose not to mention Robert just yet, it was too much for her mom to handle at once.)

"Mom, I care about you, and I want to ask you a favor. Please, get yourself some professional help, because I am not in charge of giving you a life. If you kill yourself, that will be your responsibility, not mine."

"You are so ungrateful and selfish after all I have done for you, and you're leaving me here all alone. And you don't even care if I live or die."

"I'm sure you believe that, mom. Do you want to tell me anything before I leave?"

"Yes, that this is probably the last time you will see your poor old mother. I'm going to kill myself this time."

"I'll call 911 then, because suicidal people need help."

And that's when I approached the telephone, and my mom went after me, to stop me.

"I don't need 911, I need you."

"I hear what you're saying, but I'm leaving now, mom." And then I left.

Then she told me the following:

"I could hear my mom sobbing when I left, but when I walked through the door with my suitcases, I cannot describe the feelings of freedom and joy I experienced. It was hard. Terribly hard. But now, in my own apartment, I feel so full of joy. And as it turned out, my mom didn't commit suicide. After that, every time I visit her or talk to her on the phone, and she mentions anything that's meant to make me feel uncomfortable, like "You're selfish," or "You're leaving your poor mother all alone," or "I'm going to kill myself," I hang up, or I turn around and leave. Over time, our conversations have become more normal, and I am actually starting to enjoy my mom's company a little bit more."

People sometimes get stuck in the "Why are the abusive people in my life like that?" I hear comments like these:

"Why does she have to be so rude to me?"

"Why does my boss have to be so negative about my work all the time?"

"Why does my child talk to me like that?"

"Why does my husband verbally abuse me like that?"

"Why is that person so obnoxious to me?"

And they think that because I'm the expert I'm supposed to know everything. Why abusive people are like that? ... there are a thousand possible reasons for their behavior. It could be that they are unhappy with their lives and feel a need to take it out on someone, or that they have some sort of undiagnosed neurosis, or that their sugar levels are out of whack, or they were abused by their parents as a child or a dog just peed on their leg. I don't know the answer, but I don't need to, because the reason for their behavior is not the right question here. The right question is, "WHY do you put up with it?" That's the same way we don't overthink why bees choose to sting us and die in the process, we just accept the fact that they do, and we move our arm somewhere else without questioning.

I recently read and inspirational saying that made me very upset. I had a bad reaction because I realized that there was some truth in it. I will share it with you, but I suggest that you sit down because you won't like it either.

WE TRAIN OTHERS HOW WE WANT TO BE TREATED... AND THEN WE COMPLAIN.

I told you... It's almost painful... but it's true.

You can even speak up to religious leaders

When I was a teenager, I had an experience in which I had to speak up in a major way. It was one of the first times that I realized how manipulators will say or do anything to get their way with you. Back when I was in Catholic school, around the 8th or 9th grade, I noticed that the cool, pretty, popular girls were always whispering about meeting in the afternoon's religion class where only the cool, pretty and popular girls were allowed.

That particular evening class had nothing to do with my school (complete different religious order), and I witnessed a couple of times a nun getting furious when she accidentally heard my classmates planning their evening meetings: "I don't want to hear a word about it while you are in this school!" I guess they couldn't ban us from going because it was none of their business what we did after school. The fact that the nun didn't want to hear about it, and that the cool, pretty and popular girls went there, was more than enough to catch my interest.

I inquired and asked my mom to take me there. And there I was, taking more religion classes. Nothing out of the ordinary at first, and everybody seemed really nice and welcoming. Looking back, what those particular priests wanted from us girls had nothing to do with us being cool, pretty or popular, but had more to do with us coming from families with money, because those families could donate their money to their congregation. I didn't realize this back then, but they didn't know that I wasn't from a rich family. My parents worked their butts off to get my siblings and me into good reputable and pricey schools. But I also knew there were some very wealthy girls there, with crowds of bodyguards waiting outside the school during class hours.

So, I started going to these classes. As time went on, I realized that they were demanding much more from us than would be expected. After a few weekend retreats, and a long two-week summer camp, I was getting overwhelmed. I realized that there was something wrong with the way they were teaching us religion. The leaders were deliberately making us feel bad about ourselves and lowering our self-esteem at the speed of light. It was all about guilt and obligation. They carefully chose their bible quotes to manipulate us. Though they never physically abused me, I was not allowed to be myself, but instead what they wanted me to be.

I tried to break free from them. Then they made the cool, pretty, and popular girls from my high school try to convince me to keep going to their meetings. It took a while but I left, and both my parents supported me.

Later on, I learned that many of the other girls hated it there as well, but stayed out of guilt. As it turned out, the leader of that particular congregation ended up being accused of pedophilia. When I learned that, I felt even better about getting out when I did.

Considering all of that, it's important to remember that you shouldn't just ignore your feelings if you notice something "strange" from someone who supposedly is very important, very virtuous, or very well known. Your instincts are usually right. Remember the Milgram experiment; don't let your sense of right or wrong be overridden just because someone in a position of authority tells you otherwise.

Interesting fact: *I have had clients who also feel trapped in their particular churches. Yes, intelligent and professional adults end up being trapped in a situation that gives them incredible amounts of stress and guilt because they think they are betraying God by simply deciding to quit this or that particular church. I've seen it more times than I would like. Sometimes I can help them, and sometimes they refuse to come back to see me because somebody talked them into it.*

The strangest case I've had was simply a phone call in which a guy called me with a horrendous attitude and wanted me to explain to him why my work wasn't tied to the devil. He didn't even want an appointment, just a confrontation and an explanation ... ipso-facto. I handled it gracefully and I told him that I would be very happy to see him for a free consultation so the devil and I could answer all his questions. He hung up and I never heard from him again.

Should you speak up if your abuser is ill?

This is something that my clients ask me: What if the person who abuses me is mentally or physically ill? Should I still put up with it?

Anne Katherine, the author of *Where to Draw the Line: How to Set Healthy Boundaries Every Day,* talks about this woman named Siobhan, whose mother has Alzheimer's and who was also really mean to her.

Siobhan wants to be a good daughter and picks up her mom every Monday to take her for lunch, but she has to put up with her mom's complaints and criticism. Her mother always made her feel bad about herself and she'd end up hating Mondays. The she'd stuff herself with candy and sweets to numb the pain.

She finally learned to set boundaries with her mom. One Monday, she was driving her to the usual restaurant while her mom started criticizing her.

Siobhan stopped her and told her: "If you are going to be like this, I'll take you back home. I'm not willing to put up with your criticism." To her surprise, her mom stopped. They even had a nice lunch together. Then, one hour later, at the grocery store, her mother made a cruel remark. Siobhan grabbed her mom's arm, left the basket, and took her out of the store.

"What's going on?" Her mom asked.

"I'm taking you home; you were rude to me, and I told you I was not going to put up with it."

"I didn't mean it."

"I'm still taking you home."

The mother argued for a bit because she still wanted the groceries, but Siobhan didn't give in. And to everybody's surprise, her mom stopped being critical.

The author says that as the brain deteriorates, one's ability to learn, process, and remember decreases. Still, she's been amazed at how people with all sorts of physical or emotional conditions will repeat a behavior that is rewarded and stop a behavior that costs them something they want.

"Never accept abuse. The cost is too high, and the other person is never benefited."

How can this information be useful?

This information is meant to be a reference if you feel you need to stand up to somebody. Plan your dialog in advance instead of waiting to be furious, because if you do, you can become very aggressive and hurtful in your words and behavior. Put yourself in the shoes of the person who is manipulating you and write down all the responses that he or she may tell you. Cover all the possibilities, just like I did with Bugs, and add some drama to your predictions, so you don't get caught off guard.

Remember that you don't have to have a comeback for every argument that they present. The fact of just acknowledging that you heard them ("Yes, I hear that you want me to drive you to work tomorrow,") and using the broken record technique ("But from now on it's going to be impossible for me,") will help you, even when facing the best debaters in the world.

Chapter 14

Stretching the Gap

"Whatever we plant in our subconscious mind and nourish with repetition and emotion will one day become a reality."
Earl Nightingale

They key to success is to get used to leaving your comfort zone. My friend Alana is obsessed with order and cleanliness. Her house is so clean and organized that it seems like nobody lives there. A little fuzz on the floor will make her stop what she's doing and go pick it up. I personally would never have noticed that fuzz. I like nice hotel rooms when you first arrive and everything's clean and organized. I like the crisp look. But the order and organization don't last, because when I open my suitcase I start throwing stuff everywhere.

I love it when I have my house in perfect order. Let's say I rank the order a ten. When the house is a ten, without my realizing it, I start throwing stuff around until it's closer to an eight. Eight may not be what I love, but it's what I'm comfortable with. When do I start organizing again? When the mess reaches level five, when I open a closet and things fall out of it. A five makes me uncomfortable, and there is something inside of me that won't let me rest until I've returned the closet to an eight-like condition. Ten would be ideal, but eight is good enough. When my home organization is between six and eight I'm fine, because those are the conditions that I'm used to.

Alana thinks that my home is a complete mess, because for her, anything less than a perfect ten is completely unacceptable. A hoarder, who may be comfortable at a one or two, will probably only clean when it reaches a zero-like condition, where a zero may mean having rodents in the house. And sometimes even then, it's possible that they won't do anything about it. For me, having a rodent is beyond unacceptable. For Alana, having her house in the same condition as mine is intolerable.

Our subconscious mind gets used to being in a range for just about everything in our lives: money, food, number of friends, happiness, etc. If we go outside that range, a part of our brains sets off a little alarm inside us that will make us do something to return conditions to that range. If my house is in a ten-like condition, it triggers my auto-adjust instincts, causing me to toss my purse, jacket, and keys anywhere when I come home. Those ranges are completely different for everyone else.

Let's look at a different example. I have a client who tells me that when he gets two thousand dollars of extra cash, he starts spending it until he ends up with five hundred dollars. When he has only one hundred dollars, he feels the pressure of having too little, and feels extra motivation to get more clients. When he reaches five hundred dollars again, he feels comfortable and the motivation stops.

The problem we all have, when it comes to setting goals, is that if there's no crisis that creates a commitment on our part, our chances for success become much lower. And we often feel like there's no crisis because our subconscious mind is comfortable with the status quo.

A couple came to see me. They were desperate because their seventeen-year old son refused to go to school. He watched TV all day, he didn't want to work, and nobody could make him go to school. They told me that they were constantly telling him about how worried they were about his future and that he didn't show any sign that he cared. All he would do was roll his eyes and keep on watching TV. There was no way to force him to go to school, and they needed my help.

"What would happen," I asked them, "if he brought home three girlfriends his age to live with him at your place?"

"What?" they said. "We would never allow *that!*"

"But what would happen if after you told him how much you dislike having those girls there, he still didn't do a thing, and rolled his eyes at you and didn't care? There would be no way to make him get rid of those girls and you'd just have to live with it."

As I said that, I could see that the couple were getting a little agitated. They were both on the same page, knowing that they'd do *ANYTHING* to make those girls leave the house. As they put it, "We'd have to be crazy to allow *that* type of behavior. Having girls in the house is *not* an option."

"But having the boy watch TV and not go to school *is* an option, right?" I responded.

They looked at me with puzzled expressions. I told them the story of Bugs and how, eventually, the person being annoyed will speak up, but the problem is that she waited too long to finally do something about it. The sooner we take care of what's needed, the better your emotional and physical health.

"If you treated your son not going to school and watching TV all day with the same urgency that you'd treat him with three girls in his bedroom, the boy would have returned to school weeks ago. The problem is that you are wishy-washy about responding to this situation, and letting him stay at home is easier for you than doing something about it. Having three girls in the house would give you the sense of urgency that you need."

My point was this: In order to make changes in your life, you need to pursue your goals with the right amount of urgency. And that means that you couldn't sleep, breathe or think about anything else because you'd be obsessed 24/7 with accomplishing your goal. Because the thought *of not having it is absolutely unbearable.*

Here's another example. Mary Ann goes to a job interview. Unfortunately, she's used to hostile work environments and ugly offices. This company is different, though; the offices are really pretty, and her potential co-workers seem nice and friendly. When the interview is over, she thinks: "This place is beautiful, the people here seem nice, but there's something about it that just doesn't feel right." That 'something' that just doesn't feel right is the subconscious mind telling her that leaving her comfort zone is scary. "What's the catch?" she wonders: At least in a mean environment she knows what to do, she has experience there, what if here there is an unpleasant surprise? She will want to work there, but she won't make it there because she'll sabotage herself. It's not what she knows.

The million-dollar question is: how to solve this problem? You have to get used to the idea that change will make you feel uncomfortable at first, but that every day the discomfort will be less and less.

The last part of this book has two letters: a love letter and an intention letter that have to be read at night. At night you are tired and your brain waves are similar to the ones people have when they are in hypnosis. Therefore, your mind is more receptive. So, make an appointment with yourself to read the letters. Set an alarm, let's say at 10.30 PM, or whenever you turn off your lights. This should remind you of the most important appointment of the day: your personal well-being exercise.

The first time you read it you will reject its message, you will feel uncomfortable and you will think that it won't work, not for you. Still, one part of you will like it.

"What? Me? A masterpiece? No way!"

Don't worry about the rejection. When you were a toddler and you felt great about yourself, there were probably times that you did something that drove one of your caregivers crazy and they told you something like, "Stupid, useless little child!" Back then, you looked at that person and thought, "What? Me? Useless? No way!" You knew better, those were the times when you kissed yourself in the mirror and smiled at your reflection. Back then *you knew* you were important and worthy.

But through repetition and shock over the course of your life, you started to believe something else. Of course you couldn't say that you were a masterpiece out loud! Didn't they teach you to be humble? Nobody would actually call themselves a masterpiece! They'd have to be crazy to do it! But then *you heard them* call themselves stupid and you learned. And before you knew it, you started reinforcing those neural pathways that confirm that you're not good enough, that you are broken, that you are not smart enough, capable enough or good enough. You forgot how to love yourself, and your mirrors don't receive kisses any more.

What we are doing here is reversing your everyday way of thinking and convincing yourself that you are a masterpiece. We will stop feeding the neural pathways that hold the "not good enough" belief, and we will feed, reinforce and boost the old neural pathways, that you once had, to reinforce the reality of who you are: a magnificent creature.

When you read your love letter and your intention letter, you don't have to believe what you are reading at first, and you won't because you are challenging your belief system. Don't worry about believing on it or not, just do it! When I was potty training my dog Camila, I didn't believe it was going to work. But the book said: *just do it*. Repetition, repetition, repetition. And before I knew it, my puppy was ringing the bell.

The first day you read it, you will feel that you are being extremely vain or silly and that the love letter doesn't know what it's talking about. The second day will be the like the first day, and you'll probably wonder if you are simply wasting your time. But remember, five minutes a day is not a waste of time. Just give it a chance.

The third day will be like the second day, but for some reason, you'll start seeing some familiarity in the words you are reading. You may think it's because you have read the letter for two days already, and that answer's not wrong, but it's not the only answer, or even the most important one. I've got news for you: familiarity is a good thing. It means that those little neurons are starting to realize that you are working on something big and are becoming more receptive.

The fourth day, you'll feel a little bit more familiarity, and something else. You will feel a trace of joy in your daily interactions. But you'll probably pass it off as a coincidence. The fifth day? You'll think, "What the hell. If I have been doing this for almost a week already I may as well just keep on doing it." And you will keep on doing it.

By the tenth day, you should start feeling happier, and when you look at yourself in the mirror, you will SMILE!

From day eleven to day twenty, you will feel almost the same as you did on the tenth day, which is a very good sign that your brain has started to accept this state as the new comfort zone. You will also notice that your mental self-harassment has slowed down. At some point between the twenty-first and thirtieth days, you will start beaming. That's when you will see a much bigger connection between the words that you are reading and yourself. You will probably wonder why you ever thought you were anything less than that wonderful, but guess what? So will other people. They'll start asking about you what you have done because you look great, or they will mention that there is something in your eyes and your smile that tells them that you are into something important, and you are into something important, very important:

YOU!

At some point between days thirty and forty, you will even start to speak up. Somebody will make an innocent comment that you would have disregarded in the past, something like: "You know, this team is kind of mediocre." That's when you will snap, "What? **We are** not mediocre! **We are** hardworking and smart!"

Or maybe your child will say something disparaging, or your husband will dismiss your efforts to make a nice dinner. You will find yourself saying: "If you don't appreciate my cooking, you can feed yourself next time."

I cannot predict your future, because your situation may be different than what I am describing above. Maybe your husband/wife/colleagues/bosses/children are already nice to you. But regardless of your unique circumstances, you will feel better about everything in your life, and you will stand up for what is important to you more than you ever have. You will see the beauty in yourself, and that will allow you to see the beauty in others. You will realize that this is a nice feeling and you will love it.

Then you will think that you are done and you will stop reading your love letter. "Mission accomplished" is the feeling you will have.

Even then, I will ask you to *please keep on reading it*

If you don't like the letter in chapter 15 write yourself a new one, with different traits or a different tone, as long as it makes you smile. But don't stop, get out of your comfort zone and do it. Why? First of all, because you are bombarded by negativity. That killjoy co-worker probably won't stop making depressing comments about the team right away, and that unappreciative friend or relative won't stop bugging you. People's negativity will chip away your joy, little by little.

Also, remember that you are wired to pay more attention to the negative than to the positive, even if people are nice to you on a regular basis.

Working on your self-esteem is like any other form of exercise: You are in shape when you exercise, but you fall back out of shape when you stop. The good thing is that, after weeks of repetition, what was a chore will become a habit, so it will be easier for you to change course when you find a negative pattern in your internal self-assessment.

When I am in love, or when I am in a situation that brings a lot of joy to my heart, I tend to stop reading my love letter. Then when the guy breaks my heart, or somebody gives me a bitter criticism, or I feel incredibly embarrassed about something, there I am again, back at square one, feeling devastated, shitty and totally worthless.

Then I remember, "My love letter! I forgot about it!" And in less than two weeks, I'll recover, because I am just re-awakening the neural pathways that were already there. Don't let yourself settle. Allow yourself to experience the magic that a healthy self-esteem has to offer.

Interesting fact: *People ask me if I have encountered clients who cannot be hypnotized. People assume that shy and quiet people are the easiest to hypnotize due to their docile and accommodating nature. The opposite is true. The more flamboyant, extroverted and outspoken the person, the easier, the faster and the deeper in the hypnosis they will get. It's more related to their trusting versus cautious nature than to their personality. My clients who do sales as a way of living are by far the easiest. They fall asleep in my hypnosis chair before I say anything, all I have to do is wake them up one hour later and they leave thinking I'm a miracle worker.*

Chapter 15

Let the Mental Programing Begin!

"Honestly, sometimes I get really fed up of my subconscious - it's like it's got a mind of its own."

Alexei Sayle

At the beginning of this book, I explained how your brain tends to sabotage the *I want* part of your identity because your *I am* wants to maintain its integrity. Therefore, in order to achieve what you want, you have to change your *I am*, so you can achieve the *I want*.

Working on your self-esteem is highly recommended for two reasons:

1. Your self-esteem will naturally go down if you don't do anything about it.
2. If your self-esteem is down, you will probably sabotage any goals you may have.

This chapter includes two letters for programming your subconscious mind:

The first one, to keep your self-esteem high, is designed to convince you that *you are* important and that *you deserve* good things. It will let you become the kind of person you need to be, to achieve your favorite *I want.*

The second one is your intention letter, designed to convince you that you already have what you wish for, so your RAS will make you focus on the situations aligned with your goals.

"Luck is when preparation meets opportunity."
Seneca

Your intention letter will give you the preparation, and your RAS (radar) will give you the opportunity.

These two letters are meant to help you become happier, but what makes people happy differs from person to person. As such, I recommend that you alter the letters to help yourself feel more comfortable. For example, my example says that "I am sexy", but if saying that about yourself feels awkward, you can delete it or change it to something else that you like better.

I had a client whose hypnosis included the phrase: "I'm the CEO of my life." He didn't like it because his definition of CEO was arrogant and unscrupulous. After I changed it to "I am a masterpiece" he loved it.

Another client hated the 'masterpiece' concept because it sounded too new age, but he loved the 'CEO' part.

Change the words to make your heart happy. There's no right or wrong, as long as you only use positive and uplifting words. If what feels good is something negative or self-deprecating, please refrain yourself.

Step 1

Read your love letter every night before bedtime for one month. After one month, add the intention letter to it.

A love letter to yourself

I (your name here), am a very valuable human being. I love myself so much, and I am grateful for my health, my life, and the people who love me. I am unstoppable when it comes to accomplishing my goals. I dress nicely and I take care of myself. I treat myself as the most important person on the planet ... because I am. That doesn't make me vain. On the contrary, feeling great expands my heart to make more room for the people around me. Loving myself helps me love others and love life as well. Loving myself makes me a good person who makes sensible decisions. I take good care of my body, because I love my body. I take care of my mind, because I love my mind. I take care of my soul, because I love my soul.

Loving myself makes me smile, and when I smile, good healing chemicals are released into my body to make it thrive. A happy body thrives. A happy mind thrives, a happy soul thrives. Loving myself allows me to say 'no' when I need to, and allows me to take care of myself lovingly. For every time that I say 'no', I am saying 'yes' to something else. Therefore I have the right to say 'no' as I please, because I choose where I focus my energy.

When I look at myself in the mirror, I automatically say 'HELLO MY LOVE!' while I smile. I am very important, and I know it. I have always known it, but I forgot. Now I remember.

Life is good. In the past, I chose to pay attention to the negativity, because my brain—which is worried about my survival—does that automatically. But now I realize that I am safe; we are not living in prehistoric times in which I have to be on the lookout for danger. I am not trapped in a tribe that will kick me out if I don't comply; I am absolutely free, free to express myself. I am free to choose what to wear, what to eat, and how to live my life.

I live in a community and my community is diverse. Therefore, if somebody doesn't approve of my style or my choices, I can live with that because I approve of myself. I like myself. I love the way I talk, the way I come across, my personality, my poise. I love the way I smile, I love my wit and my creativity.

Sometimes it's hard to face rejection, but the worst rejection I can face is my own. I realize that I am completely true to who I am, and that it doesn't matter if some people don't approve of me or my lifestyle or my choices. I am not on this planet to win a popularity contest; I'm here to live a full and rewarding life.

I don't delegate my self-worth to others, because it is my responsibility to take care of it. Just as I don't ask others to trim my toenails or to decide how much I should exercise, I don't ask people to tell me what they think I'm worth. I determine that for myself every day.

I am on this planet to live fully and to feel great about myself. Why? Because I have talents, I have gifts that are given to me to make this world a better place; those talents are like pearls that have been handed to me. Those talents, when used, make life wonderful and fill my life with joy. My talents, my dreams, and my wishes are important. They are mine, and I love them. If somebody doesn't approve of me, I can deal.

If for some reason I feel down, I remember that I have the power to control my thoughts. There are many reasons why people feel down. Maybe I am hungry, tired, or a little dehydrated. In the past, I thought that if I were down, it was because my life was a mess. We naturally look for explanations. But sometimes we don't have access to all the information and can't identify the real reason why we feel down.

When I'm feeling down, I know that it will pass. But I also know that my worth as a human being and my talents remain intact. Sometimes, I may even fail, but it's OK, failures make me a scientist, every failure is valuable feedback. Failure is not failure, it's feedback. Feedback is good; it's experience, it's a lesson.

Feedback makes me more knowledgeable and it has nothing to do with who I am. I am a masterpiece, a wonderful human being; I am funny, smart, creative, lovable, caring, witty, and charming. That has nothing to do with other people's opinions and has nothing to do with me being a little grumpy sometimes; it has nothing to do with the feedback I receive when I try something new.

I pay attention to my inner dialogue at all times, and just like a puppy making a mess, if that dialogue starts getting negative or messy, I can easily redirect it into something very positive and uplifting. I take myself as a whole with open arms, with love in my heart. I realize that loving myself with all my heart is the best thing that has happened to me. I deserve it, and now I can spread the joy and the love to all around me.

I love myself very much, I'm important and worthwhile, and I treat myself with kindness and compassion.

*   *   *

Continue to read this letter every night for as long as you can, and pay constant attention to your inner dialogue throughout the day. The moment that you actually come to feel that way, you are ready to take the next step: Programming yourself for what **you want**. Read your love letter to yourself for at least thirty nights before you proceed to the next step.

Step 2

Mental programming to work on the *I want*: Your intention letter.

"When the student is ready, the teacher will appear."
Buddhist Proverb

WHEN YOUR SELF-ESTEEM IS HIGH … YOU WILL BE READY

Since everybody wants different things, this programming has to be completely customized to your needs. Please answer the following question in order to create your intention letter:

What do you really want?

Describe it as it had already happened. What would my everyday life would look like? What would my routine be like? What would people around me say? How would I feel?

Let me give you an example. I ask my client Martin: **What do you really want?**

I really want to be able to speak up in meetings without feeling nervous.

Describe the ideal scenario in present tense. You have to add emotion to your words and avoid the words *I want.* For the subconscious mind, those words have no value whatsoever. Replace them with *I am* or *I feel* or *I know.*

Martin: *"For me, the ideal scenario would take place during a meeting with my boss, his peers, my peers and the VP of the company. I want to speak up and share my ideas clearly, in a confident way, while feeling very calm."*

Me: *"Pay attention to your choice of words. You cannot say, 'I want,' you have to say, 'I am.'"*

Martin: *"I see. I am able to speak up and share my ideas."*

Me: *"How do they react?"*

Martin: *"They react in very positively."*

Me: *"Describe the whole scenario as if it was already happening."*

Martin: *"The VP tells his secretary to take notes about what I just said, while everybody else is looking at me and smiling, and I feel very good and proud of myself."*

Me: "How would you like to feel when sharing your ideas?"

Martin: "Ideally, I'd like to be very calm, looking everybody in the eye, sharing my ideas in a very positive way, and explaining the details in a way that makes sense to everybody."

Me: "What else would you like to happen?"

Martin: "I would like to speak up when I don't agree. Last week, the team manager wanted an external consultant to help us with the project, but I knew I was able to do the whole task myself from beginning to end. I ended up saying nothing and being pissed at myself about that.

Me: "What would you have said?"

Martin: "I would have loved to say something like this: "Your idea to hire an external consultant is really good, because he will help us stay on track and he will make sure that we finish the project on time, but when I am leading the project, I can delegate all the legwork. I know for sure that I can keep track of everything."

Let's combine all these ideas:

Whenever I, Martin, am in a meeting with my boss, his peers and the high-level staff, I express my opinions in a calm, loud, clear and confident manner. They all respond in a very positive and cheerful way, and I feel happy and optimistic. The VP tells his secretary to take notes about what I just said, while everybody else looks at me and smiles, and I feel very good and proud about myself. It is very easy to do, and I love saying what I know. My experience is valuable, and I have a point of view that is appreciated most of the time. If it's not appreciated, I don't care; the truth is that I appreciate myself so much that I don't need others' approval. I see myself talking clearly to my peers, and I'm very proud of myself for being so brave.

*   *   *

Anita is a twelve-year-old girl who is into gymnastics. She's really good, but one of her classmates tends to tease her a lot. Despite the fact that she is very pretty and talented she feels very insecure now that her body is starting to change and she thinks she's very ugly. She wants to please her coach, and every time she receives feedback about how to do better she feels like a failure. She would like to feel pretty and to feel confident when she performs. She would like to speak up to that girl Irina and she would like to have her coach's approval. I crafted this letter for her.

I, Anita, am one of the best gymnasts in the area. I perform like an angel and I spin in the air like a feather. When people see me perform they realize that what I do is impressive. Still, for me it's easy and fun. It's like my body moves by itself in a graceful and beautiful way.

I feel happy that I have a natural talent, just like my mom and my sister. Despite my talent I'm also very resilient and hardworking.

There's something that I also do very well: Get angry. I used to be afraid of Irina but now I'm not. Now she is afraid of me! If she teases me, I get angry and I yell at her to leave me alone. I know how to defend myself because I'm strong. I like to hear my voice loud and clear. I am important, I am pretty, I am powerful, and I am an amazing gymnast. Now that I am brave, all my classmates want to be my friends; I am becoming popular. But it's not about their love and acceptance, it's about mine. I love myself and I accept myself. I live peacefully and happily because I know who I am and I love myself. Nobody messes with me any more.

My body is changing and it feels alien sometimes, but my body is an evolving miracle and I'm like a caterpillar becoming a beautiful butterfly. I welcome the changes in my body with love and acceptance.

I am loved by my parents and my siblings, I have good friends, and my coach is proud of me. People like me. But what's most important is that I like myself even more.

* * *

Marina needs the discipline to go to the gym, she needs to stop watching soap operas in the morning and get moving. That lifestyle has made her gain a lot of weight because as she watches TV she eats, even if she's not hungry. She doesn't want to once again buy clothes one size larger. She needs to do something and now.

Her letter is something like this:

I Marina, I love myself very much. I am athletic and disciplined. I love going to the gym and I always have time for it. When I'm at the gym I feel energized and happy. Every day I have the following routine:

I wake up at 7, have my coffee and some yogurt and I get into my gym clothes.

At 7.30 I drive to the gym, and I work on the treadmill from 8 to 9 and I do some weights from 9 to 9.30. I hired a trainer and he helps me once a week. In just a few days I'm able to feel the difference in my body and in my mind. I have stopped the negativity and I have more energy and joy than ever. I love myself and I treat my body with love. I'm careful about what I eat and I absolutely love eating healthy. My goal isn't to lose weight; my goal is to get my body moving, to give it healthy food on a regular basis and to treat it with the utmost love and respect. My body is a masterpiece. The end result is energy and weight loss.

Soap operas in the morning? No way! Not me! Not anymore! I find them awfully boring and annoyingly dramatic. I stimulate my mind with something more productive like reading a good book or taking a class. Sometimes during 'those days of the month' I have cravings and I get moody. Those days I am even nicer to myself and I treat myself even better.

In a few weeks my life has changed for the better. I love myself and I'm proud of myself.

* * *

Remember that your letter has to be happy, positive, in present tense and written in a way that makes the mind believe it has already happened. When you write your own letter describing what you really want, remember to do it in present tense, as if it were already a fact of life. If you write it as if it is about something in the future, you will be always chasing it, and if you say it in a negative way, you will confuse your mind. You have to make it positive, present and full of as much emotion as you can.

For you, I wish no less than what I wish for myself, no less than what I wish for my children and all my loved ones. For you, I wish a life full of magic. I hope that this book helps you bring a little more magic into your life. I'll finish with a quote from one of my favorite authors:

> "I've been fortunate enough to have some amazing experiences in my life so far. I've trekked to one of the highest base camps in the Himalayas, meditated with Tibetan monks in the Dalai Lama's monastery, earned my US Army Infantry patch, walked 550 miles across Spain, lived in Paris, been the only non-black, non-woman member of the Black Women's writers' group, written a novel, held the hands of dying patients, and worked with some of the best people in Silicon Valley. But the most transformative experience has been the simple act of loving myself."

> Kamal Ravikant, Love Yourself Like Your Life Depends on It

> Now go forth, and learn to love again.

Another book from the same author:

"Think Like a Picky Eater and Never Diet Again."

The recipe for disaster is loving food so much.

People on diets spend more time thinking about food than picky eaters do. The more they think about something, the more they want it. The more forbidden something is, the more they want it. The more they want to avoid a certain food, the more they see it in displays, in magazines and in stores. People on diets run into forbidden foods all over the place, as though life was playing a mean joke on them.

Picky eaters may not have the best eating habits, but they have something that people on diets don't have: Interests and passions that are not food oriented. They don't remember when was the last time they saw a cheesecake at the grocery store because when buying groceries they were in a hurry to leave, so they stuck to their list while making plans for the next hike with friends. Picky eaters don't need to keep an eye on what they eat because they see food as fuel.

Acknowledgements

I would like to give my thanks to all the people who have allowed me to give life to this project.

To my sons Ivan and Fernando, the joys of my life, for letting me share their anecdotes in this book, for being my guinea pigs and for making each of my days incredibly fun.

To Jared Levy for your support, suggestions, and patience, and for always helping me with my English.

To my parents Alba Rached and Rafael Alamillo, my sister Rocío and my brother Rafa.

Many thanks to Elaine Andrews, for her eagle eye, input, suggestions and encouragement.

To all my patient, thorough and hardworking editors: Jerome Levy, Judah Frankel, Paula Correnti, Felicity Doyle, Otha Cole, Brenda Green, Azucena Vega and Jessica Katz.

To Jay Polmar and his team of professionals.

To Danielle Lakin for the beautiful book cover. You captured the idea so well, that it was really hard for me to choose one from all the covers you sent me.

To Heroud Ramos for creating the perfect cartoons to bring my ideas to life.

To Azucena Vega, Vero Rena and Rodrigo Juarez for their unconditional support from beginning to end.